STRONG
in the
SPIRIT

BY James Lee Beall

The Adventure of Fasting
Strong in the Spirit

STRONG
in the
SPIRIT

JAMES LEE BEALL

Wanda Wilson, Editor

Fleming H. Revell Company
Old Tappan, New Jersey

TO
my son James
Strong in the Spirit?
You bet your life!

Library of Congress Cataloging in Publication Data

Beall, James Lee.
    Strong in the spirit.

    1. Christian life—1960– I. Title.
BV4501.2.B387   248'.4   74–32467
ISBN 0–8007–0729–X

Contents

1
Perfection

Deep breakdowns in individual lives are being experienced by many people today. Life has become too much for them. They are confused and unhappy because they are not mastering life. Instead, life and circumstances are mastering them. Something has snapped inside and it has left their lives dangling at loose ends. They have real problems that must be resolved.

Is there help for them? Is there a way to master life? Can we sit on top of life and enjoy living? The answer is an emphatic *yes!*

In the Bible, we have these words of Paul to Timothy:

> And if a man also strive for masteries, yet is he not crowned, except he strive lawfully.
>
> 2 Timothy 2:5

What is Paul talking about? Striving for the masteries of what? The apostle is talking about masteries in your life and mine. He is telling us that there is a way to master life and to be above every problem.

I do not say there is a way to master life so there will be no problems. I am saying there is a way through Christ, who is the way to total meaning in life, where, in spite of the troubles and difficulties which do arise, we do not lose the sparkle and the will to live. Through Christ, we master life and do not allow the problems which are a part of life to master us.

Life must be a single unit—a whole. It must have total meaning, for without it, it is a total mess. When life does gain total meaning, it lights up with significance and purpose.

Too many people lack the essential central cohesion—that lasting cement in their lives which can hold them together in the face of any problem. When they are struck by sorrow, disappointment or temptation, they go to pieces. They cannot stand up under the blows which life deals to everyone. They don't know how to take it. This should not be and it need not be.

Consider the appalling increase of nervous disorders. More than half the hospital beds in this country are occupied by patients suffering from mental and nervous disorders. The economic losses due to these disorders amount to over a billion dollars a year.

If there were statistics available on every individual who suffers from some sort of mental illness or nervous disorder, the figures would be staggering. These people never enter a hospital but drag themselves about their tasks while they are inwardly defeated and at war with themselves. They are only half alive and are making only a 50 percent contribution to life. They are cancelling themselves out with inner conflicts.

Excluding Yourself   The first and foremost part of life which must be mastered is the part of you that will not turn unreservedly to God. Many people do not turn to God and serve Him because they themselves have deliberately excluded themselves from Him. They do so on the pretense that they are just not religiously inclined (as though that had anything to do with it). No one in the whole wide world is spiritually inclined!

You will notice that the phrase *religiously inclined* was deliberately changed to *spiritually inclined*. The world is full of religious people but not many among them are spiritually alive —so do not alienate yourself from God because you do not feel spiritual. This is a self-imposed limitation. Shake it off.

Understand that in the sight of God everyone outside of Christ is spiritually dead, does not know God, and cannot understand His ways. You are no different—so don't use this as an excuse to exclude yourself from the fellowship of God. Come to

God today. Tell Him, in prayer, what your life has become. Hide nothing. You are the kind of person whom the Lord God delights in helping and healing. Remember, Jesus said:

> Come unto me, all ye that labour and are heavy laden, and I will give you rest. Take my yoke upon you, and learn of me; for I am meek and lowly in heart: and ye shall find rest unto your souls.

Matthew 11:28, 29

Take yourself off your own hands with a full self-surrender into the arms of Christ. Say, "Lord, here I am. I am sick of myself. I don't know what to do with myself anymore. Take my life into Your hands, O Lord, and make it a new one."

Once you have made a full surrender of yourself, become receptive to Christ's forgiveness and grace. Receive Him. Receive His forgiveness. Receive the witness of the Holy Spirit into your life, assuring you of your acceptance by the Lord God. Here is where mastery in life begins!

Premature Perfection   Now that you have placed your life into the hands of Christ, by His Spirit and His Word (the Bible), He will begin to lead you step by step. Right at the very beginning, it is absolutely necessary to master the strong desire for immediate perfection or premature perfection.

Don't attempt to become perfect overnight. It won't happen. Be careful about the goals you set for yourself. Don't set unattainable goals. Be realistic. Often, people set goals for themselves which are so high they cannot possibly reach them and, when failure comes, they fall into a tailspin of despondency. Trying to live life at a level not yet attained will wear you out. Jesus Christ taught that life in the Kingdom of God, as well as life in the natural, is a process of gradual growth.

God does not plant trees; He plants seeds. When you are born again into the Kingdom of God, you are like a seed. Christ explained this principle very carefully in the parable of the Sower. He said:

9

... He that soweth the good seed is the Son of man; the field is the world; the good seed are the children of the kingdom. ...

Matthew 13:37, 38

The Lord God does not expect fruit from seeds. That comes later. However, He does expect us to be faithful today, to be what we are.

He that is faithful in that which is least is faithful also in much: and he that is unjust in the least is unjust also in much.

Luke 16:10

Three Basic Attitudes   There are three basic attitudes which are necessary if we are to master life and the human urge to attain premature perfection.

1. Don't be in a hurry to do too much too soon. Live a day at a time. Be faithful today. Grow a little today. In this way, you will be ready for tomorrow.

2. Be modest and humble in accepting facts. If someone knows more than you do, admit it readily. Don't bluff your way through life. This is one of the severest blights the Christian church has suffered. The church is filled with people who are spiritual bluffs. They have failed to be honest with themselves and cannot be honest with others. They will not face up to the true facts concerning their relationship with God and with others.

3. Be zealous. Give your all to God and to life. Live life. Don't be afraid to be an active part of life. Don't sit back and watch it go by. Take part in the real issues around you. This is what living is all about.

While Waiting for Perfection   There is another very important attitude that must be added to the three already mentioned—the personal attitude toward imperfection.

There are many people whose lives are completely stymied

because these individuals are waiting to be perfect before they do anything about it themselves. If we wait for perfection, we will wait from now until doomsday!

When I first began to minister on the radio, I could hardly tolerate the sound of my own voice. When I listened to the replays of the programs, I was appalled at the number of mistakes I made. For a while, it almost got the best of me. Almost —until one day, the Lord spoke very plainly to my heart, "Why are you seeking such perfection on the radio when you do nothing else perfectly?"

Understanding dawned upon me. That word brought me freedom. I knew I could continue to serve God in my imperfection while I was striving for the mastery in the realms of speech and thought. This was one of the most important lessons I learned.

It is also the reason why I have continued to broadcast for these many years. I believe I do things better than I did when I began, but I know I still do not do things perfectly. However, I will not wait to be perfect before I do things. Nor will I wait until I do things perfectly before I do them. That would be waiting for the impossible.

I can remember reading the story of a man who was cutting down a tree when a friend approached him and asked him what he was doing. His reply was, "I am building a house, but today I am only cutting down a tree." Building a house is a gigantic, time-consuming task, but the first step toward that goal is cutting down the tree—today. Tomorrow, a few boards can be made. In its own time, the house will be completed.

It does not pay to look too far into the tomorrows. We must learn to live with ourselves and our imperfections today and continue to strive for the mastery. Perfection will come, but only gradually. It is a day-by-day process.

Bargaining With God   This same truth can be applied to money. In almost every church we find people who would be glad to contribute some of their money to God if He helped them to become millionaires. Do you know that more "religious" people have been taken by confidence men than any

11

other group of people? Nominal Christians will invest in one scheme or another in an attempt to bargain with God. They say, "If the Lord will bless this financial venture, I will give twenty percent of it to the church." Such words are mere religious talk used to cover a heart full of avarice.

God makes no bargains with anyone. He does not need the dollars of the rich for His Kingdom. The Kingdom has always been supported and always will be supported by those who give of what they have now.

Christ commended a little widow for giving her mite, because she gave what she had and did not wait to give from an abundant supply she did not have and for which she was hoping (*see* Mark 12:42–44). We must *do* with what we have now.

This is the beauty of tithing. Whether a man makes a thousand dollars a week, or a hundred, or ten, if he gives his 10 percent to the Lord, he is sharing equally. He is giving what he has now. He is not waiting for a million dollars before he gives anything to the Lord. The Kingdom of God is supported by people who give dollar bills, not by those who give thousand-dollar bills.

Changing Ourselves   If we set standards for ourselves and others which are too high and out of reach, we will settle down to doing nothing. The Lord waits patiently for us to grow and develop. We must also learn to be patient. Learning this one truth has helped me a great deal.

Because we cannot change the world today, we often refuse to change the changeable situation presently at hand. The consequent result is that we begin to slip from perfectionism to pessimism. This easily provides an excuse for us to become apathetic. Actually, we have no right to think of changing the world unless we do all we can to change ourselves and the situations around us.

The healthy reasoning of Jesus was seen in the fact that while He proclaimed an absolute order, the Kingdom of God, He was willing to sit down with individuals to lead them to individual changes.

You have tried to live life by your own rules and standards

and have found that it hasn't worked. It's time now for you to begin to master life and observe God's rules. If you don't, life and circumstances will continue to master you. The decision is yours.

2

Conversion

A woman of considerable beauty and talent requested an appointment and, when she came to see me, she let me know in short order that she was leaving her husband and three teen-aged children. I knew this family and was stunned by her announcement.

I asked her, "Why? What has happened?"

Her reply was, "No one will listen to me! I have talked, suggested, yelled, stomped, and done everything I know to do, but nothing ever changes. I quit."

Her face reddened and she almost left my office when I said, "If you can't change them, how about changing yourself?"

"I don't need to be changed. They do."

I said, "You need conversion."

"I'm saved," she said. "I've been a Christian for years."

"Yes, you've had your sins forgiven and have experienced good and needful change but a deeper conversion is needed. You, as a person, need personal conversion."

Our conversation continued along these lines until she became like a little child instead of an all-knowing, world-arranging mother. Her ways and attitudes were wrong and she was getting nowhere fast. To recognize and admit that she was wrong was a tough thing to do; but when she did do it, the change began, and in the process, the family became changed also. It works.

Life demands that we be changed before we start changing the world. Instinctively, we endeavor to conform the world to our image. We know it will be a complete distortion of what it ought to be but we go on just the same. Every person must master the desire to conform the world to his ends. We must face up to life and identify ourselves. We are human beings and not God. Playing God is exhausting, and besides that, we are not qualified for so great a task. The universe will not back us up.

Our world is filled with people in deep mental and spiritual trouble because they can't arrange the universe to suit them. They feel all would be well and everyone would be happier if people would only listen to them. These are the world-arrangers. They are unhappy people. They need conversion.

The Life Principle   All life is based on the principle that if it is to be healthy, it must think in terms beyond itself. This is true of the basis of all life—the cell. We are told that all cells, when they come into existence, are capable of becoming the whole—but they must renounce this idea and surrender themselves to being differentiated portions of the whole in order to serve the entire organism. In that renunciation, their purpose is realized. They lose their lives to find them again.

When cells refuse to serve the organism and try to become the entire organism—try to make the rest of the cells serve them—what is the result? A cancer—a group of unsurrendered cells trying to become an entire organism by making the surrendered cells serve them. It is a group of cells that has become self-centered. The cancer eats its way to its own death and to the death of the organism upon which it feeds. It has broken the law of being. It has not played according to the rules. Death is the result.

Every organ and cell looks to something beyond itself, and by doing so, it finds itself. It becomes a part of the whole organism. In the same way, each person must get himself off his own hands and start at the right place—with himself. He must cease trying to change people and begin serving them instead. This is the way to change other people. These are the rules of the game of life. Heed the advice Christ gives:

14

At the same time came the disciples unto Jesus, saying, Who is the greatest in the kingdom of heaven? And Jesus called a little child unto him, and set him in the midst of them, And said, Verily I say unto you, Except ye be converted and become as little children, ye shall not enter into the kingdom of heaven. Whosoever therefore shall humble himself as this little child, the same is greatest in the kingdom of heaven.

Matthew 18:1–4

Do you desire to enter the Kingdom of God? It can't happen without change—conversion. We must be changed and the result of the change causes us to *become as little children.*

Conversion Means Turning   Christian conversion is: a new direction—*be converted;* a new spirit—*become as little children;* a new sphere of living—*enter the Kingdom of God.*

We cannot face up to life and master it without being converted. "You must be born again" (*see* John 3:7). There are no two ways about this. This is the starting place. If you want to master life, be converted. It is as simple as that. God's rules for the game of life are established. The starting point is conversion.

To master life, you must find a new direction. The word *converted* comes from *con* meaning "with" and *vertaire* meaning "to turn." So the word *conversion* literally means "to turn with."

But why should I turn? Turn toward what?

Turning involves a decision. Is your face or your back toward God? The first step in the new life is to turn your face toward Christ. You do not make that turn alone—Christ is there helping you in this turn, the moment you throw your will in His direction.

Christ helps you to do what you can't do for yourself—to break with the old life—but the decision to turn must be your own. No one can decide for you—not your parents, not your associates, not your husband or wife, not even God. You stand alone. As a free moral being, you must make the decision alone,

15

severely alone, but the moment you make the decision, Christ is with you! From then on, you are no longer alone and never will be.

When you break with your old life, you become as the little child Jesus called unto Him. Think of it! You are promised a new spirit—the spirit of a little child—the wonderful knowledge and assurance that you are given a fresh beginning. You are made free from your old guilts and from that feeling of estrangement from God. You begin your new life by being obedient to the ordinance of water baptism. The Bible says:

> Then Peter said unto them, Repent, and be baptized every one of you in the name of Jesus Christ for the remission of sins, and ye shall receive the gift of the Holy Ghost.
>
> Acts 2:38

In the waters of baptism, the Lord God will deal with your inner heart and will give you a new spirit.

I Played God   This new spirit or attitude is the part of conversion that is avoided by most people. In my youth, this was my personal area of difficulty. I did not want to become a little child. I wanted to be free to make my own decisions. As a young man, this was very important to me.

With the advent of World War II, I wanted to become involved in the military. This was not only an opportunity for adventure but it was also a means of getting away from home and living my own life. I wanted God to get me home safely and I told Him I would appreciate this, but I also desired that He keep His distance. (Don't crowd me, Lord!)

I didn't mind God being God over a world I had no ability to touch or influence but I wanted to be god over my own personal world. I felt I knew more about myself and my world than He did.

I worked hard at being god of my life for a few years but I couldn't make a go of it. I kept messing up. Eventually, after all kinds of disasters, mental strain, and deep frustrations, I surrendered my dumb attitudes and became converted (changed) in my spirit.

I had known for a long time that I was like a little child who didn't know his way around and was forever getting lost, but I would not admit it. When I finally did make the admission, the weight of the world slipped from my shoulders to Christ's shoulders. I have since left the world, both general and personal, in the hands of God—where it belongs. I had to become a little child and put my trust in my heavenly Father.

When you *enter the Kingdom of God* and gain a new sphere of living, your circumstances will not change but you will now live in two worlds at once: the world of physical relationships and God's world. God's world makes new the whole outer world. You will now do things with a new motive, a new spirit, a new outlook. Your whole reason for living will be changed.

A New Creature   In Christian conversion, you will find you are given a new nature along with a new desire, a new direction, a new sphere of living and a new quality of living. Conversion is not reformation. It is regeneration. The most striking description ever given of conversion is this one:

> Therefore if any man be in Christ, he is a new creature: old things are passed away; behold, all things are become new.
>
> 2 Corinthians 5:17

This is where the mastery of life begins. Conversion changes you and the change takes place where it is needed—deep down inside.

You must always remember that all of our human urges have been perverted by sin and, through conversion, they are converted to Kingdom ends. So conversion is turning *from perversion*. Although the urges remain as an integral part of us, they are now turned toward new ends with new motives and a new spirit.

Conversion does not dehumanize us by transplanting an alien life into the framework of the natural. Conversion, for example, does not take away sexual desires as many strange religious people teach, but it does cause lust to pass away. It makes the marriage relationship new and what it ought to be.

The warring instinct which was so destructive and disruptive has not passed away, but its energies are channeled into constructive areas. It now fights for causes, for human rights, for the oppressed, for justice, for the right to minister the Gospel of the Kingdom. Conversion will not make a Casper Milquetoast out of you. Rather, your drives will be directed to where they ought to be. You will be happier, livelier, more full of natural spontaneity and freedom than ever was the case.

Surrender Yourself　　　The answer for many of you today is this deep conversion. Get your inner life changed and the whole world will look entirely different to you. Start with yourself.

Many people are like the extremists we see around the country who will demonstrate for the causes of peace while at the same time they are burning down buildings. They are endeavoring to accomplish something on the outside of them that isn't the fact inside. Young people turn to drugs to escape the realities that persist in the outside world, only to find it is their own inside world that is making them so miserable.

Life will leave you *on the shelf* and will refuse to use you if you do not stop demanding change in others. Do not merely add God to what you now have. In the Bible, we are warned not to "put new patches on old garments" or "new wine in old bottles" (*see* Matthew 9:16, 17). This means when you deal with the Lord God, you must empty out completely and start brand-new! If you do not, you will end up in a greater mess than the one in which you now find yourself. Change your direction. Do not expect God to change His!

3

Secondhand Religion

Secondhand religion is much like having someone do your courting for you. When I met my wife, Anne, I wanted to be with her and have my own firsthand encounter with her. In fact, I did not want anyone else around. I knew what I knew about her because I had been with her myself. Having someone tell me about her was not enough.

This is precisely the way it is with the Lord. It is one thing to have someone tell us about Him and quite another to have a personal encounter with Him.

The majority of people who call themselves Christians have a religion of the secondhand variety. This is highly regrettable since such a religion is without the ingredient of life. Christianity, if it is to be an effective force in our lives and in society, must be a firsthand matter—a personal relationship with the Lord God, as the Apostle John said:

> That which was from the beginning, which we have heard, which we have seen with our eyes, which we have looked upon, and our hands have handled, of the Word of life; (For the life was manifested, and we have seen it, and bear witness, and shew unto you that eternal life, which was with the Father, and was manifested unto us;) That which we have seen and heard declare we unto you, that ye also may have fellowship with us: and truly our fellowship is with the Father, and with his Son Jesus Christ.
>
> 1 John 1:1–3

In these verses, John is describing firsthand religion. He personally had seen Jesus Christ. He had heard Him. His hands had touched Him. He knew what he knew because it was a knowledge he had gained by firsthand contact. The purpose of his

19

writings was to tell others that they, too, could have such a firsthand contact which would bring them into fellowship with the Father and His Son, Jesus Christ.

All that is done and taught in the Church of Jesus Christ should bring people into a real and personal relationship with Christ. Unless this is achieved, religion is in vain.

Religion cannot be only creeds, rituals, books, services, and prayers. It must be much more than that—a personal union and communion with Jesus Christ—or we have a secondhand religion, one that is only hearsay!

The Sons of Sceva   In the Book of Acts, we read an account of first- and secondhand religion. We are told about the ministry of the Apostle Paul in the city of Ephesus and how the Lord God worked with Paul in a supernatural and powerful way:

> And God wrought special miracles by the hands of Paul: So that from his body were brought unto the sick handkerchiefs or aprons, and the diseases departed from them, and the evil spirits went out of them. Then certain of the vagabond Jews, exorcists [people who supposedly drove out demons by using secret names], took upon them to call over them which had evil spirits the name of the Lord Jesus, saying, We adjure you by Jesus whom Paul preacheth. And there were seven sons of one Sceva, a Jew, and chief of the priests, which did so. And the evil spirit answered and said, Jesus I know; and Paul I know; but who are ye?
>
> Acts 19:11–15

The man who had the evil spirits had a firsthand experience with them but the seven sons of Sceva had only a secondhand knowledge about Christ and were no match for the evil spirits.

Imagine them saying, "In the Name of Jesus whom Paul preaches. . . ." They had no personal experience of the power of the Lord nor did they have a firsthand contact with Him, yet they endeavored to use His Name because Paul had used His Name. This sounds all too familiar. Many people in the church try to use powers that do not belong to them. They never became heir to them!

One of the most amazing facts in this story is that the demons knew more than the sons of Sceva knew. The demons in the oppressed man knew Christ and, most certainly, they knew Paul who preached Christ. You can rest assured that the demons know everyone in the Kingdom of God who has authority and power over them!

Firsthand Preaching   If the Name of Jesus Christ is to exert any power, it will not be through secondhand knowledge. It cannot be by the Christ who is real to somebody else. Christ must be real to the person who uses His Name.

You see, secondhand religion is always overpowered by firsthand evil. The comparative impotence of the church today is due to the secondhand nature of its religion. Too many who preach Christ do not preach the availability of Christ.

The Christian world is filled with joiners—people who attach themselves to a person or a religious system and ride the coat-tails of the individual or denomination. I am reminded of a young minister who came to see me to inquire about entering the field of radio broadcasting. He wanted to know how I did it, how the radio ministry was supported, and how the bills got paid. He asked questions concerning direct mail, appeals, literature, the answering of mail, and so on.

Finally, I interrupted him with this question, "What are you going to preach and what do you have to say?"

His answer was very vague but he seemed to give me the impression that he felt if I could do it, so could he. This could very well be true but this was not a good enough reason. He had no business being on the air simply because I was. Every person must know for himself exactly what the will of God is for him personally.

It doesn't happen often, but occasionally I have the opportunity to hear some of the Gospel programs on the air around the country. One need not listen long to discover whether the speaker is speaking from firsthand or secondhand knowledge. Some who quote Moody, Spurgeon, Finney, or Wesley, have nothing to offer but what these men preached.

They have no personal, firsthand knowledge of the saving grace of the Lord Jesus Christ. They do not know truth for themselves. Those great evangelists of past years were great in the Kingdom of God but they are not to be our source of authority. Our authority must come from firsthand knowledge!

I refuse to preach in the Name of Christ whom Moody preached. I must, of necessity, preach the Christ whom James Beall knows! If I do not have a personal knowledge of Christ, then I have nothing to preach.

The Woman of Samaria   When Jesus Christ spoke to the woman of Samaria (*see* John 4:5–42) and revealed to her the secrets of her heart, she knew she had run into God. She received a firsthand knowledge by this encounter. She said, "He told me all that I ever did."

Because of her firsthand testimony, many Samaritans believed in Christ and beseeched Him to stay with them for a few days. The Lord accepted the invitation. For two days He taught them and, hearing the words of Christ, many more Samaritans believed. After their personal encounter with the Lord, they went to the woman who had first told them of Him and said:

> . . . Now we believe, not because of thy saying: for we have heard him ourselves, and know that this is indeed the Christ, the Saviour of the world.

> John 4:42

The people of the Samaritan village passed from the secondhand realm to the firsthand realm in these words. It was no longer a matter of mediated faith; now it was an immediate faith with nothing between.

The greatest necessity of the church today is the conversion of secondhand Christians into firsthand Christians—a conversion from walking in half-light to walking in full light.

What Makes the Difference?   The difference between firsthand and secondhand religion is the redemption that is ours in Christ Jesus and the coming into our lives of the precious presence of the Holy Spirit.

You will agree when I say the Holy Spirit has been estranged in a large measure from modern Christianity. It presents a Holy-Spiritless Christianity—a demand without a dynamic. In recent months, I have been told by people who have been brought up in the church from early childhood that in all that time they never heard a single message on the power and presence of the Holy Spirit within the human life.

Not too long ago, I heard the account of a Roman Catholic priest who became very hungry for reality—hungry for the firsthand religion which he had read about in the New Testament.

Carefully and prayerfully, he began to seek for the Baptism in the Holy Spirit. First, he prayed a prayer from his prayer book which was titled: *Come, Holy Spirit, Come.* Nothing happened. Then he realized he was praying somebody else's prayer. This was not his own prayer, therefore, absolutely nothing could happen. He began to speak to God out of the depths of his own heart with no mediator but Christ. God heard him! Not only did God hear him; God filled him with the Holy Spirit!

I had a mother speak to me about her son who was in his late teens. She wanted me to hire him, give him a job at the church and she would secretly pay his salary. She was convinced that if he would be with me eight or ten hours each day, he could stay "saved" and would not get into bad company.

Naturally, I told her *no!* Every person must learn at some time or another to stand on his own two feet. This young man must have a meeting with God for himself and he must be the one who desires to serve God. The boy must have a personal firsthand meeting with Christ or else he will spend his life hanging on to someone for strength and support.

The Lord can speak to each and every man who desires to hear. It is much easier to have someone do this for us but there is nothing that can take the place of firsthand encounter.

Without the Holy Spirit   As we read in the Book of Acts of the work of the Holy Spirit in the early church, we see a

23

dynamic in operation which literally propelled the church. It was hard to differentiate between the activity of the early apostles and the work of the Holy Spirit. It was a combination that was inseparable.

Stop for a moment and consider this thought. Suppose there had been no Holy Spirit. What kind of Christianity would have been passed on to the world? It would have been the four Gospels without the Upper Room experience, without the coming and power of the Holy Spirit.

The disciples were afraid of the future in spite of the Resurrection of Jesus Christ and remained behind closed doors. The news of the resurrection stirred them emotionally, but they were completely powerless and spiritually unprepared to stir the world and their generation. This required the gift of the Holy Spirit.

Without the coming of the Holy Spirit to the early church, we today would have only a hand-me-down Gospel story, a secondhand religion. With the coming of the Holy Spirit (God's Spirit), the Lord God has taken up His abode within us—the only place where it counts.

Unfounded Fear   When I speak of the Holy Spirit bringing us a firsthand religion and putting us on a firsthand basis with Christ, I am made aware of the fact that many people would love to have this experience but they are hesitant about it because they have been gripped by fear.

Somehow they have become afraid that the Holy Spirit might make of them a strange person and would cause them to do strange things. This is a totally unfounded fear; it is not true in the light of New Testament Christianity. Actually, the Holy Spirit leads us into truth and teaches us how to live well-balanced lives. He leads us into right paths!

A woman came to see me to question and argue about the Baptism in the Holy Spirit. She felt I was quite wrong in saying that the Baptism in the Holy Spirit was another personal meeting with the Lord. Didn't I know this had all been done the moment I had my sins forgiven—and there was nothing more to receive?

I told her of my own experience of meeting the Lord and

what the Holy Spirit Baptism had meant to me. The Holy Spirit was not a thing—and I had not received a nebulous something by having this experience. Being filled with God's very own Spirit was a personal, firsthand experience for me.

She questioned me over and over again regarding this meeting I had with Jesus. The Jesus she knew was a historical figure who lived centuries ago. As she continued the discussion, she began to relent and I could sense she desired meeting the Lord in a new way. I asked if she would like to have me pray with her. She immediately responded by saying, "Yes, by all means."

As I laid my hands on her head and began to pray, I could strongly sense the hunger of her heart. In a moment of time, the Lord was baptizing her in the Holy Spirit and she was glorifying the Lord in a language she had never learned. When she left my study, she was a knowledgeable woman who knew what firsthand religion was all about. This is what makes the difference.

Good Balance   The Bible uses the terms *Holy Spirit* and *Spirit of Jesus* interchangeably. Actually, they are one and the same. This is well illustrated in the Book of Acts.

> They made their way through Phrygia and the Galatia district, since the Holy Spirit prevented them from speaking God's message in the province of Asia. When they approached Mysia they tried to enter Bithynia, but again the Spirit of Jesus would not allow them.
>
> Acts 16:6, 7 PHILLIPS

This truth is more important than it appears on the surface. It is important because too many people have inferred that the Holy Spirit is something strange and off-center. This is not so. The Holy Spirit was poured upon Jesus Christ without measure and He was the best balanced and poised man history has ever known. The Holy Spirit working in Jesus Christ was real sanity.

This is one of my strong premises in preaching the Gospel. It is my firm belief (and something which we must strive to attain) that we can have the fullness of the blessing of the Holy Spirit with sanity and good balance. Today, men have been made to fear the work of the Holy Spirit because of the extreme emotionalism and unbalance of some who claim to be led by the Holy Spirit.

Christ, Our Example   Again I say, look at Jesus Christ. There was nothing psychopathic about Him. He never acted as though He were walking in a dream. He did not go off into a trance and see visions and dreams. Jesus received guidance for His life through communion with the Father in prayer. He was in full control of His faculties at all times. He was well balanced, sane, and poised. In fact, His character was perfectly balanced.

If we are filled with the Holy Spirit, we will be like Jesus Christ. We, too, will receive our guidance throughout life by the direction of the Holy Spirit. If we are not like Him, then we are not being guided by the Holy Spirit but by some other spirit.

The Holy Spirit led Christ into a firsthand relationship with the Father. There was nothing secondhanded about His union with the Eternal God. For this reason the Holy Spirit has been given—that we might know the Lord God firsthand. The Holy Spirit is a gift of God—there is no experience like it in all the world.

Allow me to ask you a straightforward question. Have you received the Holy Spirit since you believed? Do you possess a firsthand religion? Don't settle for anything less! Christ came that we might have a firsthand relationship with the Father.

4
Mistakes and Blunders

Most people dislike making decisions. Many would rather swim the Atlantic than make clean-cut decisions about themselves and life. If they could turn this part of their life over to someone else, they would be relieved and happy. Christians usually would like to have God pick up for them at this point.

God does not and will not make decisions for you. He will set alternatives before you and often make your choices relatively simple ones, but the final decision will be yours.

Our aversion to decision-making can be traced to a deep inner desire to always be right. This is totally impossible. No one can be right all the time. Everyone must face up to life at this point. You will make mistakes and blunders.

Before God ever made us, He knew we would make mistakes and blunders. Settle this fact in your mind. God made man as a volitional creature and not as a programmed computer. Given the ability to choose, God knew man could choose and make a wrong decision and this is exactly what happened. Man's error in judgment did not catch God by surprise. The Lord knew that He must everlastingly deal in grace if He created man with the freedom to choose his own way.

None Perfect Let us at this point accept the fact that there is no perfect person in the universe. None is perfect but God. You are not perfect and neither am I. Presidents, ministers, and priests are not perfect.

One of the duties of the pastoral ministry is to remind people that we who minister the Gospel of the Lord Jesus Christ are human and we do make mistakes. We dare not allow anyone to harbor the mistaken notion that we are some kind of gods. Yet, there are some who assume that ministers should be perfect and when they see that we have feet of clay, they want to crush us because *they* have been crushed. They presupposed something to be true that would not stand up in a real world. When their concept of the clergy is shattered, their minds will not accept the true facts. Having been hurt, they want to hurt back.

The Searchers We also have among us those who expect the church to be a perfect society. I have seen people come to our local church, the Bethesda Missionary Temple, to see if we are the perfect local church for which they have been searching.

They soon find out that we are not. If they stay around long enough, they will become aware of our deep devotion but they will not find us a perfect people. Consequently, they will soon be on their way, continuing their search for the perfect church. Their quest will be in vain for no such church exists this side of heaven. In fact, if a perfect church existed, it would immediately become imperfect the moment these searchers stepped inside.

You have heard people say, "I would not be found dead in that church. There are too many hypocrites there." Exactly. There are hypocrites in every church. The church has always been a society of the imperfect. The *true church* is a church within a church—a remnant within a professing, believing body. It has always been this way.

If we stopped worshiping and serving until we were perfect, we would have a long wait. We are men who serve men. We are imperfect people who serve imperfect people, but we are joined to a perfect and a living Christ who can take our imperfections, our mistakes and blunders, and make them work together for our good and for the good of the Kingdom of God.

Mistakes and Motives   During our lifetime, we are faced with many decisions, many of them distasteful, and each time there is the possibility of making the wrong decision. Although that possibility may frighten us, we dare not draw back from life and decisions because of the fear of being wrong. Always remember, the Lord, in His dealings with us, looks into our hearts. He weighs our motives as well as our actions.

Are you aware that God judges sin, mistakes, and blunders in their own light and does not lump them together and consider them the same? Sins are one thing. Mistakes and blunders are quite another.

There are times when we all set out to do a good thing and end up making a big mess of it. Making a mess of things is not sin! Sin is judged by the motive. The Bible definition of sin is:

Whosoever committeth sin transgresseth also the law: for sin is the transgression of the law.

1 John 3:4

Therefore to him that knoweth to do good, and doeth it not, to him it is sin.

James 4:17

These Scriptures tell us that sin is to know good from evil, right from wrong, and to willfully act contrary to what we know is right. Mistakes and blunders do not fall into this category.

A good way to clearly illustrate the difference is this rather simple picture. Mother is busy around the house. Her little son wants to help her. We know she can do things much better without his help but she dare not discourage the boy's initiative, so she allows him to help.

His first task is to bring the milk from the porch. As he lifts the bottle, it slips from his hand. Milk and glass fly in every direction! Should he be spanked or disciplined for this? Certainly not! Why? Because he was attempting to do a good thing. The motive of his heart was right and sincere. He did not willfully set out to break the bottle. If that were the case, it would be a different matter. He did not sin. He made a mistake. He blundered. He tried but he failed. This young fellow should be told the difference at this point.

This is the way God deals with us. He weighs the motive. He looks into the depths of our hearts. This makes the difference between sin and mistakes!

Rising Above a Problem   I learned this lesson a number of years ago when the opportunity presented itself and I agreed to lead a team of ministers in a number of important crusades in the Union of South Africa. The money was raised, equipment purchased, passports obtained, visas were approved and we were set to go.

Just a few days prior to leaving, we received a letter from the South African Embassy cancelling our visas and entry permits. Racial strife had broken out and the government would no longer permit large gatherings of people. What we had proposed to do could not be done. We had made a mistake. We had chosen the wrong time. I was in conflict.

For a number of weeks and months, I was depressed and

ashamed. I imagined what people were thinking and saying. One day, the realization came to me. What did I expect? Did I think I could go through life without making a mistake or a miscalculation? This was foolish and unrealistic thinking. I was human. I had made a blunder. I had not sinned. If I turned the situation over to God, I knew He could make it work out for my good.

As I knelt before God, I made certain I was in His presence. Then, I confessed the fact that I was a human being capable of making mistakes and I had made a big one. I also resolved to prepare myself more thoroughly before getting involved in any further ventures. After I had done this, I placed myself and the entire situation in the hands of the Lord and walked away from it.

Looking back, I thank God for His hindrance in this matter. My inexperience and youthful desire to minister in Africa had warped my good judgment. To put it simply, I was not spiritually prepared to do what I had contemplated.

A House Divided   When there are things which must be done and decisions to be made, we must gather all the facts together and then act. I had not done this. When we have carefully examined the problem or situation, it is imperative that we act upon it. It is damaging to allow ourselves to be tormented by fears and worries about whether or not we will do everything exactly right.

Fears and worries about making mistakes and blunders will drive us into conflict, and this is ruinous. To be at our best, there must not be any inner division or conflict. Christ said, "And if a house be divided against itself, that house cannot stand" (Mark 3:25).

Christ did not say the house *will not stand.* He said it *cannot stand.* Contrary to the nature of reality, inward division brings inward disintegration. We are told that at the basis of every nervous breakdown there is a conflict.

The idea has been explored that people break down from overwork, but overwork is *not* the cause of a breakdown. The cause is the inability of an individual to cope with emotional conflicts. The nerves and the body, in general, can stand almost anything provided there is inner harmony and the absence of conflict.

Perhaps you are sitting in a prison of your own making because you have made a serious mistake. Maybe it was a deep moral mistake or, perhaps, a deliberate sin. Don't sit there and whip yourself and allow the inner conflicts to grow day by day. Take your sins and problems to the Lord God. He will forgive you and then you must forgive yourself! He can and will make life not only bearable but meaningful as well.

Since conflict is the only thing that causes breakdowns, there is only one cure for it—the surrender of that conflict! The conflict must be discovered, revealed, and related to the rest of life.

You must learn today that you cannot allow conflict to get inside of you. When you make a mistake, when you blunder, or even when you willfully sin, take the matter to God. Surrender it immediately. Do not beat yourself over the head with it. Do not labor under self-condemnation. Do not let guilt ruin your life. Surrender it all to Christ!

Making Decisions   Everyone makes mistakes. The biggest mistake we can make is to ignore this fact. We will make some wrong decisions during the course of our lives but this should not make us afraid of life.

To avoid making decisions is worse in character result than an occasional wrong decision. We learn through our mistakes. An occasional wrong decision may do some harm in a particular situation but indecision weakens the whole body and character.

Do not endeavor to look too far into the future when faced with making a decision. Make your decision on the basis of moral principles and leave it there. After you have decided what to do about a problem, let it remain decided. There may be occasions when a decision must be reversed but let that be the exception rather than the rule. Useless regret over a wrong decision is more harmful than a wrong decision made honestly. Do your best and leave the rest.

God can and does overrule a wrong judgment that is made honestly. He can bring good out of it for those who love Him. The thing in itself may not be good, but He will make it work for good.

31

Christianity does not offer an escape from the mistakes, blunders, and suffering of this life. It is not an escape from reality. Christianity is Christ dwelling within us in the person of the Holy Spirit—to make us equal to all the problems, mistakes, and sufferings of this life.

When the Bible says that we are more than conquerors through Jesus Christ our Lord (*see* Romans 8:37), it means that through Him we come out of every problem and difficulty with a little something left over. We come out of every scrape with our resources intact, ready for the next skirmish with life.

We who are in Christ never run away from life. We face the worst it has to offer and we are able to turn it into great victories. We can do it because Christ has already shown us how to do it. He faced the cross, the worst death a man could die, and He turned it into a glorious victory—the salvation of the world.

5

Inadequacy and Inferiority

"My life has been a mistake. I just can't seem to do anything right. I'm a disappointment to my family, my wife, and my children. Sometimes I wish I had never been born."

A young executive spoke these words. This man had an excellent position, was making good money and seemingly had everything going for him, but he was falling apart on the inside. Life was too much for him. He did not feel he had the inner resources to cope with life and its pressures and did not know what to do.

When he talked with me, he expressed great concern because his company was considering him for a promotion and he was afraid of it. He wasn't sure he could handle it because he did not feel equal to what would be required of him. His self-esteem would not allow him to realize that he was a competent individual.

People who suffer and do not realize their full potential in life because of feelings of inferiority and inadequacy manifest negative responses to intellectual, emotional, social, and even physical demands. They are inept, use poor judgment, and have difficulty in adapting themselves to rather simple life situations.

Very often they will express a strong need to cling to others for support or they will go to the opposite extreme and display an exaggerated independence in which they attempt to deny their dependency needs and will steadfastly refuse help from everyone.

I am reminded of a story I once heard. A man went to a psychiatrist seeking help for the terrible inferiority complex which had gripped him. The doctor examined him thoroughly and requested that he return the following week. On his next visit he asked, "Doctor, do I really have an inferiority complex?" The doctor replied, "No, you don't have an inferiority complex. You're just inferior."

Often, this is the case with us. Our inferiority is not a complex, it is a fact. God knows this. In calling us, He has called us to perform tasks which are beyond our own natural ability—that we might discover His strength. This is why Christ is the answer to all who suffer from inferiority.

We *are* inferior and a complex is natural, but through God, our inferiority is neutralized and we learn to develop right attitudes because of our association with Him.

The Foolish and the Weak   A careful, thorough study of the Bible can cause us to feel inferior because the Lord God has called us to do and perform that which seems much too big for us. For example, the Lord commands us to go into all the world and preach the Gospel to every creature (*see* Matthew 28:19).

This is a big order. It can't be done. Commands such as this could easily give us an inferiority complex. To add insult to injury, God also says:

> For ye see your calling, brethren, how that not many
> wise men after the flesh, not many mighty, not many

noble, are called: But God hath chosen the foolish things of the world to confound the wise; and God hath chosen the weak things of the world to confound the things which are mighty; And base things of the world, and things which are despised, hath God chosen, yea, and things which are not, to bring to nought the things that are.

1 Corinthians 1:26–28

Why would God do such a thing? Certainly He could demand top-level individuals to do His bidding. After all, He is God and who could stop Him?

Yes, God is God and He can do anything He wants to do and in His wisdom He has chosen to use common, ordinary people like you and me. In one way we are happy He has chosen us, while at the same time we are uneasy.

Why would the Lord deliberately inform us that we are called by Him in spite of our foolishness, weakness, and baseness? Surely, He knows this kind of negative psychology will add to our feelings of inferiority. God says it because it must be said. We play games and usually look at ourselves in too kindly a light. Everyone must experience a moment of truth.

The miracle of the grace of God is that He knows exactly what we are and yet He has called us. We are made fully aware that there is no good in us—but when we are in the hands of God and the Holy Spirit is moving within us, we eventually become capable of doing anything the Lord God calls us to do.

The Bible clearly informs us that we are like grass—here today and soon gone—and that we were born in sin and fashioned in iniquity, but by the power and grace of God we are made alive and able to "do all things through Christ which strengtheneth me" (*see* Philippians 4:13).

Dealing With Our Problem   The first step in mastering any problem in life is to bring it into the light, expose it for what it is and then deal with it. Do not run a bluff. If you have a problem with inadequacy and inferiority and have tried unsuccessfully to shake it off, admit your failure.

Simply say to the Lord, "Jesus, I have strong feelings of inadequacy and inferiority and they are spoiling my whole life. This is a weak area in my life where I need real help. Please help me." If you will be honest with yourself and sincere with God, you will get results.

The next step is to learn to be receptive to the resources and power of God. For those of us who cannot get it through our heads that we can be of use and value to the Kingdom of God, the answer lies in learning how to appropriate the endless source of strength available to us through the Holy Spirit. The Bible says:

> He that believeth on me [Jesus], as the scripture hath said, out of his belly [innermost being] shall flow rivers of living water. (But this spake he of the Spirit, which they that believe on him should receive). . . .
>
> John 7:38, 39

Here we discover that the Holy Spirit becomes as *rivers of living water* in the lives of believers. It is not one river but many rivers that shall flow, for the gifts of the Spirit are various and many. The water that Jesus offers us springs forth like a sparkling and bubbling beverage. It is not the dormant water of a cistern but water that refreshes and supplies us with life-giving energy.

The Day of Pentecost   On the day of Pentecost, when the disciples of Jesus (about 120) were baptized with the Holy Spirit, the Bible account says:

> And suddenly there came a sound from heaven as of a rushing mighty wind, and it filled all the house where they were sitting. And there appeared unto them cloven tongues like as of fire, and it sat upon each of them. And they were all filled with the Holy Ghost, and began to speak with other tongues, as the Spirit gave them utterance.
>
> Acts 2:2–4

This which came upon them came from heaven—from without. It was not an upsurge from the subconscious but a downpour from heaven. These people had received a gift from God —the gift of the Holy Spirit, and it put everyone on the same level. The disciples of Jesus Christ were all inadequate individuals before this experience. Now they were filled with the Spirit of God and this was the beginning of adequacy.

The Meek Become Mighty   There are some offshoots of so-called Christianity which tell us that the answer to our problems of inferiority and inadequacy is to awaken the latent powers that are within us. This is not the teaching of the Bible. Christ put the emphasis elsewhere when He told His disciples:

> And behold, I send the promise of my Father upon you; but tarry . . . until ye be endued [clothed] with power from on high.
>
> Luke 24:49

The Lord Jesus said that the Holy Spirit would come *upon you*. He did not say we would discover this power within us. It is a power from on high—not from within. This emphasis makes us God-conscious and not self-conscious!

If the disciples had been given the modern-day advice to discover their own resources, they would have been out of the race. They had no inner resources. When they were forced to resort to their own resources, they hid behind closed doors. They were totally inadequate and filled with fear.

When the pressure of adverse circumstances came upon them, one betrayed Him, another denied Him with an oath, and in the end, they all forsook Christ and fled. Even after the resurrection, they were behind closed doors because they were afraid. Discover inner resources? They would have only discovered selfishness, impotence, and fear. Modern advice would have left them cold.

Because they could not turn to themselves, they turned to the risen Christ who had promised them they would be endued with power from on high. This made things different! It opened a door, not only for them, but for every one of us. Thank God, we can all be endued with this same power. We do not have to be worthy or specially endowed or even good. All we have to do is just be willing and receptive and obedient.

The very thing that modern advice suggests we should find within ourselves was experienced by the disciples. They discovered they had a wonderful resource within them. The Holy Spirit who was now abiding in them added a plus to all they were and did.

The Apostles' First Miracle   Following their reception of the gift of the Holy Spirit, the Apostles Peter and John were walking to the temple in Jerusalem for their season of prayer and refreshing. As they were about to enter the temple gate (called Beautiful) they met a lame man begging alms. Peter looked at the man and said, "Silver and gold have I none; but such as I have give I thee: In the name of Jesus Christ of Nazareth rise up and walk" (Acts 3:6).

Peter took the lame man by the hand, lifted him up, and immediately the man was healed. Although Peter did not have silver or gold to offer to the beggar, he did have something far greater.

Perhaps the most serious inadequacy modern man can know is the inadequacy felt because of the lack of money. The hell of an empty purse is the deepest hell which modern materialism can conceive. Peter was there. He was without funds but he walked straight out of that hell of material inadequacy into the adequacy of heaven as he said, "Such as I have give I thee."

If Peter had been adequate in the material sense, he would have tossed a coin to the beggar and that would have been the end of the story. Peter was materially inadequate but he turned to the grace of God and an astounding deed resulted—the man was healed!

This is what the inner working of God by the Holy Spirit will do for us. The Holy Spirit makes us inwardly adequate to face life. Through the Holy Spirit we know we have a sufficiency within us that enables us to face up to life and master it. God's

Spirit removes the terrible sense of inferiority and inadequacy and causes us to know we can do all things through Christ who strengthens us.

More Than Believing   In the Book of Revelation, Christ said:

> . . . . I am Alpha and Omega, the beginning and the end. I will give unto him that is athirst of the fountain of the water of life freely.
>
> Revelation 21:6

To know God has resources available to us, to ask in faith, to receive and appropriate His power is what we need, but there is a marked difference in believers. Some believers only believe —while others believe and drink. Those who believe and drink know how to take and receive from God. They do not thirst or feel inadequate. Some people are always thirsty because they have done nothing more than believe. They give mental assent to Christ Jesus but they do not assimilate Him. Their minds believe but their hearts do not receive. They remain inadequate.

There are many people like this. They are zealous and ardent believers but they are exhausted. They work for God and strive to do good but have not learned the necessity of maintaining strength by drinking freely of the waters of life. They work hard and become drained. Feelings of inferiority develop because they cannot do all they would like to do.

The Prophet Jeremiah was such a person. Jeremiah had deep feelings of inadequacy and inferiority when the Lord called him:

> Before I formed thee in the belly I knew thee; and before thou camest forth out of the womb I sanctified thee, and I ordained thee a prophet unto the nations.
>
> Jeremiah 1:5

Jeremiah replied, "You are wrong, Lord. I am not a prophet. I can't speak in public. You had better get yourself another man" (*see* v. 6).

The Lord knew Jeremiah in and out. He knew exactly what his strengths and weaknesses were. Consequently, the Lord said:

> . . . Say not, I am a child: for thou shalt go to all that I shall send thee, and whatsoever I command thee thou shalt speak. . . . And the Lord said unto me, Behold, I have put my words in thy mouth. See, I have this day set thee over the nations and over the kingdoms, to root out, and to pull down, and to destroy, and to throw down, to build, and to plant.
>
> Jeremiah 1:7, 9, 10

Jeremiah's answer to his problem was God and His enabling power. The answer for all of us is God, the Holy Spirit flowing in and out of us as mighty rivers flow through the land. The Holy Spirit is the gift of God which produces spontaneity from within. It is a true gift that does not weaken us by providing too much assistance. Instead of weakening us, it awakens and strengthens us.

6
Criticism

The subject is criticism and its devastating effect upon the human personality and spirit:

> Judge not, that ye be not judged. For with what judgment ye judge, ye shall be judged: and with what

measure ye mete, it shall be measured to you again. And why beholdest thou the mote that is in thy brother's eye, but considerest not the beam that is in thine own eye? . . . Thou hypocrite, first cast out the beam out of thine own eye; and then shalt thou see clearly to cast out the mote out of thy brother's eye.

Matthew 7:1–5

These words spoken by Christ are words of caution to those who find themselves becoming critical and censorious. Christ is saying that we should give ourselves a careful once-over before we start picking our brother apart. This is better than good advice. Christ is telling us this is necessary if we are going to face up to life and really live.

The Callings of God   It is most important for us to master criticism because this is one of the very deep holes into which we can fall and if we are not careful, being critical can become a lifelong attitude. This, we do not want.

People become critical because they fail to recognize the kinds of people the Lord God calls. God deals with all of us in redemption. Every person used by God is someone whom He has changed. God picked all of us off the scrap heap. We are waste material.

Christ did not come to call the righteous, but *sinners*, to repentance. These are the only people God can use—born-again sinners. Since God uses imperfect people, we ought to stop looking down our noses at those who fail to arrive at our definition of perfection. God knows every one of our imperfections and shortcomings but He is not always criticizing us. The reason: God's attitude toward us is redemptive, not critical. There is a vast gulf between the two.

Most criticism is usually motivated by jealousy, by a sense of inferiority, by egotism which would try to lift itself by putting down the other person, by finding fault with others to cover up faults within one's self.

40

When Love Runs Low   Critical people cannot help anyone. This is precisely why criticism is wrong. If you love someone, you love him enough to help him. When love runs low, criticism runs high.

In my counseling of teen-agers, I find that most family problems between parent and child stem from continual criticism on the part of one or both parents.

Recently, a young lady came to see me to simply inform me that she was leaving home. We were friends and she wanted me to know that what she was doing had nothing at all to do with her Christian life. She would continue in the church and would love and serve the Lord but she could not and would not live any longer with her mother.

She said, "I have been yelled at, threatened, criticized until I can no longer take it. My father just sits there and does nothing. He doesn't seem to have an opinion about me one way or another. My mother, on the other hand, is at me continually.

"She tells me I must never hesitate in making a decision; I must never make a mistake; I must never be confused; I must always know what to do; I must never date a boy who does not meet her standards; I am a continual disappointment. No matter what I do, it is impossible for me to please her. I fail every time. From now on, I give up trying. I am leaving."

The critical get criticized. This is the way it is and the way it will always be. No one can live with a critical parent and grow. Inevitably, the child will seek escape, and rightly so.

Prosecutors or Witnesses   God has not called us to be prosecutors but witnesses. We cannot at the same time denounce people and announce the Good News concerning Jesus Christ. Our job is not to be judges of the earth. That job belongs to God. We must have sense enough to leave a job as important as that in God's hands. Only God is good enough and wise enough to decide people's destinies. Christ said:

Don't criticise people, and you will not be criticised.
For you will be judged by the way you criticise others,

41

and the measure you give will be the measure you
receive.

Matthew 7:1, 2 PHILLIPS

This was the secret of the ministry of Jesus Christ. When He
looked at people, He did not look at them critically, as did His
disciples. When He saw the multitudes milling around as sheep
without a shepherd, He was moved toward them with compassion. He felt for the people and this allowed the love and power
of God to flow through Him like a river.

Because of His great compassion for us, He committed to us
the *word of reconciliation.* We are to say to the world in the
stead of Christ, "Be ye reconciled to God." This is why I preach
the Gospel and leave judgment to God. It is a simple and safe
formula to follow. Remember, Jesus Christ said that with the
judgment you pronounce, you will be judged. This tells us
clearly that the person who dispenses judgment is actually laying it up for himself.

We have such *partial* knowledge of people and their motives.
We are in no position to judge anyone. We do not know the *why*
of people's actions. Only God knows that. The Scriptures tell us:
". . . the Lord seeth not as man seeth; for man looketh on the
outward appearance, but the Lord looketh on the heart" (1
Samuel 16:7).

The Circumcision   In the second chapter of the Book of
Romans, the Apostle Paul was speaking to a group of Jews who
took great pride in their nationality and in the fact that they had
received outward circumcision after the manner of Abraham
and Moses. Paul said:

And art confident that thou thyself art a guide of
the blind, a light of them which are in darkness, An
instructor of the foolish, a teacher of babes, which
hast the form of knowledge and of the truth in the
law.

Romans 2:19, 20

These particular Jews were highly critical of the Gentiles for they judged them according to the outward signs of their religion. They forgot to take into account the fact that God looks at the heart. As God looked into the hearts of both the Jews and the Gentiles, He found in some Gentile hearts a love for God which the religious Jews did not have. On the basis of the heart inspection, the Lord said,

> For he is not a Jew, which is one outwardly, neither is that circumcision, which is outward in the flesh: But he is a Jew, which is one inwardly; and circumcision is that of the heart, in the spirit, and not in the letter; whose praise is not of men, but of God.
>
> Romans 2:28, 29

Diagnosing the Ailment   The first step toward mastering the attitude of criticism is to properly diagnose the ailment. You are critical because you are out of harmony with God. This is absolute truth. It is not an oversimplification. The critical attitude toward life and people is dissolved when we get into living fellowship with God.

Did you know you can take your own spiritual temperature by an awareness of your critical attitudes? Watch it! The next time you become critical, you will find you have slipped from the place of spiritual blessing in God. When your prayer life becomes sloppy, you become critical, but when you are in close touch with Christ, your life takes on a redemptive quality, not a critical one.

Going around and picking out motes that are in other people's eyes does not sharpen our own eyesight. Rather, it dulls our eyes to our own faults. The attitude then becomes, "I must be good. Look at the bad I am discovering in others." This is a fallacy. By finding the bad, you become the bad. Always finding the bad is in itself a bad attitude. This you must master!

Where there is real communion with Christ, there are no critical attitudes toward men. When we are in tune with Christ, we have the "love of God shed abroad in our hearts by the Holy Spirit" (*see* Romans 5:5). Love makes you different. Love makes you understanding. When you are out of fellowship, you are out of love and when you are out of love, you do not want to understand—you cease to care.

If you find yourself in the throes of criticism and feel this message is meant just for you, read carefully. You can master this spirit of criticism by acknowledging it as a very real problem and carrying it to Christ. Confess it to Him openly—no holds barred—honestly, and forthrightly. If you have become critical, admit it. God already knows it. He is just waiting to hear it from you!

When you have thoroughly exposed your critical attitude before God, keep your eye upon Him and what He, through you, can do for others.

Next, stop comparing yourself with others. The Lord God is at work in your life. What He is doing for you is not exactly the same as what He is doing for someone else. You are a member of the Body of Christ, a member in particular. There is no one else quite like you. The work of God in your life is for your particular needs. Do not attempt to be anyone else. Be yourself. This is a full-time job.

Then leave the other fellow alone. Stop picking him apart. Allow the same God who works in you to work in somebody else. Step back and allow God to do great things for someone else. Every Christian should learn this lesson.

One of the most difficult facts for most of us to accept is that God *does* love other people besides us. This is the curse of denominationalism. Most denominations will not admit this but it is true just the same. The basic tenet of most denominations is that the Lord God cannot possibly bless anyone who is outside their particular denominational walls.

If you do not believe this, join up with a group and then tell the members of the group that you have decided to leave and join with someone else. You will be judged, condemned, and criticized as never before. You see, God is not the author of denominational religion and He never was. God looks into the hearts of all men and judges them by what He sees. The Scriptures tell us:

For the eyes of the Lord run to and fro throughout the whole earth, to shew himself strong in the behalf of them whose heart is perfect toward him. . . .

2 Chronicles 16:9

Barnabas   If it had been up to the apostles in Jerusalem, Saul of Tarsus (who later became Paul the Apostle) perhaps would never have become such a mighty instrument in the hands of God. Fortunately, there was one man who looked beyond the former conduct of Saul, far beyond the reputation he had established for himself. The man who did so was Barnabas.

His sterling quality was that he could rejoice when God was blessing someone else. He could rejoice and not be critical of Saul. Barnabas walked with God. This was his secret. It was said of him, "He was a good man, full of the Holy Ghost and faith" (*see* Acts 11:24). That is about the best thing that could be said about anybody.

The attitude of Barnabas toward Saul was redemptive and not critical. When no one else would listen to Saul, Barnabas sought him out. He brought Saul to the church at Antioch, Syria, ministered to him, prayed with him and for him, and rejoiced when the Lord God began to use him for His glory. This is true Christianity. We need more of it. What do you say that more of it should begin with you and me?

Negative, critical people never have a following. People will follow the positive, appreciative person! If you are critical, your friends will drop away. A porcupine is an uncomfortable bedfellow. Life will be happier and considerably more meaningful if you will cease looking for that beam in your brother's eye. There is much more to life! Go God's way, the redemptive way, not the critical way.

7

Fear

Many people are beset by a secret enemy that is responsible for much illness and suffering. Its name is fear.

In our day, a certain amount of fear is an expected, normal reaction, but when fear runs out of control it becomes destructive. It robs us of courage and cripples our reasoning so that we become frightened, insecure individuals who go through life overreacting to the slightest threat. Instead of expending our efforts to conceal our fears, we need to take a good look at them and learn to function effectively in spite of them.

There are two kinds of fears—efficient and inefficient. Efficient fear protects the individual by causing him to withdraw from dangerous situations. It is a natural fear which is directed to objects or persons which can be dangerous to life if they are regarded carelessly. At the same time, efficient fear gives the individual skill and caution in performing dangerous feats.

An act of bravery is not the result of not experiencing fear. It is the result of performing courageously in spite of it. This type of fear makes a surgeon skillful because he is responsible for what happens to the patient who is put in his care. Realizing a human life has been placed in his hands, he is fearful of making a mistake that could be fatal.

Efficient fear makes a motorist a good driver, an aviator a good flier, and a sailor a good mariner. It develops a superior skill in the performance of duty. It creates a respect and careful evaluation of the object feared.

Inefficient Fear—Anxieties and Phobias   Inefficient fear is the kind of fear that takes away skill and leads into bondage. This fear manifests itself in the form of anxieties and phobias.

In *anxiety,* we experience a warning of danger in which the specific nature of the danger is not known. Anxieties are irrational fears of accidents, illnesses, death, or insanity. They are fears without an object and are usually due to a condemning, threatening impulse within. The man who was given one talent by the Lord and did nothing with it, was filled with anxiety. He didn't know what he was afraid of but "I was afraid, and went and buried my talent in the ground" (*see* Matthew 25:25). All this man had to show for a lifetime of existence was a hole in the ground. Fear made him do this.

The second kind of inefficient fear is *phobia.* A phobia is a persistent fear of an object or situation which, in reality, does not present any actual danger to the individual. It is fear attached to objects which are not dangerous in themselves—high places, darkness, thunder and lightning, crowds, being alone, closed places, and so on.

Fear is usually accompanied by such neurotic symptoms as headaches, stomach upsets, back pains, dizzy spells, feelings of inferiority, and guilt. This is because there is some measure of frustration involved when we are forced to withdraw from a situation. Because we tend to hate the things we fear, the frustration is then accompanied by feelings of hostility toward the object or person which is the source of the withdrawal.

Expressing the hostility would only create more problems, so the hostility is turned inwardly toward the self. This kind of behavior is often incompatible with our standards and ideals and causes all sorts of physical, mental, and spiritual suffering. We are told that many illnesses such as heart trouble, ulcers, migraine headaches, high blood pressure, colitis, and even diabetes stem from fears and an unsettled attitude within. These are only a few of the physical ailments which grow from a mental and spiritual disorder.

Sickness of Mind and Spirit   In a report made by a group of Johns Hopkins' doctors, one psychiatrist said that 40 percent of the patients who came to the clinic were suffering because of something that began in the mental or spiritual realm. Some doctors put this figure as high as 80 to 85 percent. This means that a considerable number of all physical ailments can be traced to a mental or spiritual disorder. These figures are proof of the tremendous amount of bondages and sicknesses which spring from fear and other negative reactions.

You must consider two very important facts: A sickness of the mind and soul may be transmitted to the body; and the sickness of a body may be transmitted to the mind and soul.

Man is a very complex creature. The Almighty God created him with a body, soul, and spirit. Actually, when any one of these parts is touched, the whole man is affected. Consider the man who is passing the sickness of mind and soul to his body. The most common way to do this is through fear. The Bible tells us of the torment that comes to a man who gives room to fear.

> Forasmuch then as the children are partakers of flesh and blood, he [Jesus] also himself likewise took part of the same; that through death he might destroy him that had the power of death, that is, the devil; And deliver them who through fear of death were all their lifetime subject to bondage.
>
> Hebrews 2:14, 15

When a man allows the fear of death to invade his life, he is opening the door to a bondage which will hold him for his entire lifetime. Don't give room to fear. Don't let yourself become subject to fears. For when you let fear come in, you will be put under bondage.

In my time of counseling, I have seen the crippling and paralyzing effects of fear on people. One woman had a gnawing, harassing fear that her husband would die and leave her desolate. Because of this totally unfounded fear, she became grasping and selfish and would scarcely allow her husband out of sight.

She grew tense and nervous and eventually developed a chronic nervous disorder. When she saw the error of her ways and committed her husband and her future into the hands of Jesus, she was healed. You see, she could not be healed until she could take her hands off the situation.

Many people have been prayed for many times and yet have not been healed. Why? It is just that they do not and will not put their future into the hands of God. A person in this condition must root out such fears at all cost before he is destroyed by them. The way to root them out is to surrender the fears and commit your life into the hands of God. Trust God. Apply the words of David:

> The Lord is my light and my salvation; whom shall I fear? the Lord is the strength of my life; of whom shall I be afraid? For in the time of trouble he shall hide me in his pavilion: in the secret of his tabernacle shall he hide me; he shall set me up upon a rock.
>
> Psalms 27:1, 5

I know a gentleman who suffered a heart attack and though he fully recovered, he has become a prisoner of fear. Because of this one attack, he has resigned his job and sits around the house almost afraid to move, for fear he might have another attack and die. His mentality is giving way under the strain of this fear, even though his body is basically sound.

This fear has not only crippled him but it has affected his entire family. He will not come to church and because he doesn't come, his whole family stays home. Spiritual death is coming to that home because of fear. The man needs a spiritual release but he cannot be released until he commits himself into the hands of God.

Fear Thou Not   If we truly give ourselves to God, are born again of God by the Holy Spirit, and come into true covenant relationship with Him, we need not be fearful of anything. We can apply the words of Isaiah to ourselves:

> But thou, Israel, art my servant, Jacob whom I have chosen, the seed of Abraham my friend. Thou whom I have taken from the ends of the earth, and called thee from the chief men thereof, and said unto thee, Thou art my servant; I have chosen thee, and not cast thee away. Fear thou not; for I am with thee: be not dismayed; for I am thy God: I will strengthen thee; yea, I will help thee; yea, I will uphold thee with the right hand of my righteousness.
>
> Isaiah 41:8–10

Christ saw this enemy—fear—at work when He taught His disciples concerning the working of the Kingdom. In the parable of the Sower who sowed the Word of God into various kinds of ground, Christ taught them what fear can do. Some of the Word fell among thorns. Here is Christ's explanation for this:

> And that which fell among thorns are they, which, when they have heard, go forth, and are choked with cares [fears] and riches and pleasures of this life, and bring no fruit to perfection.
>
> Luke 8:14

Fears can choke out your spiritual life if you allow them to do so. Fear, anxiety, and worry can warp a man's whole personality.

Worrying About Tomorrow   A mother came into my office, harassed with a fear that her daughter would end up marrying the wrong boy. Just to show you how unfounded her fear was, the young daughter was in her early teens and as yet was not even keeping company with boys! Yet this mother was certain her daughter would marry the wrong fellow!

She said she knew this by premonition and assured me that her premonitions, at times, were very accurate. She was making her own life a hell on earth as well as her young daughter's. This mother was spending all her time on borrowed fears and worries of the tomorrows and neglecting to do the very thing she should have been doing. She should have been teaching, loving, and directing her young daughter so that when the time came for dating, she would make the right decision about the right young man. Jesus told us:

> Take therefore no thought for the morrow: for the morrow shall take thought for the things of itself. Sufficient unto the day is the evil thereof.
>
> Matthew 6:34

In other words, tomorrow will have its own problems which will have to be handled tomorrow, about which nothing can be done today. Don't borrow tomorrow's troubles and pile them on top of today's problems. Today's problems are enough of a burden for today!

Running From Fear   Our young people face very real problems and fears in this complex day in which we live. They have fears about a lack of popularity, their personal appearance, and that they might not be accepted by the crowd. Such fears have put many of them into terrific bondage. Some become slaves to these things and pursue them with all the life that's in them while others, realizing their lack, crawl into a shell and subject themselves to other bondages. Fear brings bondage!

A young man recently told me of his problem with fear. His fear became obvious while he was telling me of the difficulty he was experiencing with his parents. Actually, he felt that his emotions toward his father were anger and hatred. They were, but they grew out of an inordinate fear.

When speaking of his life as a small child, he said, "When my father would become angry with me, he would get all red in the face, clench his teeth and his fists and look as if he were going to kill me—usually over little or nothing. I can remember how I felt when my father came home from work. I wanted to hide. I ran for cover. I kept out of his way. I felt I would do something wrong or bad and he would look at me in that way. I honestly thought he might kill me."

"What did you eventually do? How did you handle the matter?"

"In my early teens, I ran away from home and all the time I was away, I was scared to death. I just knew someone who knew me would see me and tell my father. I went into hiding. Consequently, I ran out of money and had to go home. I really and truly felt I was going home to die. This would be the final blow and my life would be over."

"What did your father do when you returned home?"

"He roared and he raved and got red in the face and I got

down on my knees like a puppy dog being whipped. I thought he was going to hit me, but he didn't."

Fear almost ruined this young man. The fear of his father made him feel absolutely worthless. He felt he could do nothing right and that everything he ever did wrong would somehow be reported to his father.

Finally, this young man faced up to his situation. As I spoke to him about the love of the Lord Jesus Christ, he began to listen. I told him the Lord loved him just as he was, mistakes and all, and would make him an entirely new person if he would but yield his fears to the Lord and receive Jesus in their place.

Together we asked the Lord Jesus to come into his life and wash away his sins and with them all his fears, especially those fears attached to his father. The Lord began to do just exactly that. The fears and torments began to leave. In their place came a new confidence. Today he has a job and has discovered he is capable of performing with a minimum of mistakes. Jesus is presently washing his fears away.

Release From Fears We have discussed only a few of the fears which are doors to bondages but let's turn our attention to the answer to this crippling problem. Is there an answer? What can be done to gain release?

The initial step toward a deliverance is to go before the Lord with your fear, name it for what it really is, and admit the fact that you need help and cannot help yourself. Just to know your enemy, just to face him squarely, point him out, identify him, and call him by his right name is a big step toward deliverance. Facing the fact squarely that you are held in bondage will make you seek help for release. Too many folks won't admit it. They try to pretend the fear isn't there, but they aren't fooling anybody.

When God made Adam, He gave him dominion over all the works of His hands. After all things were created, the Lord God allowed the rest of the Creation to pass before Adam so that he might name the creatures. Notice this: Adam had no dominion over any creature until he first named him!

Name your fear and God will give you dominion over it! Expose your fear for what it really is and you will be given mastery over it. Surrender your fear into the hands of God, remembering that every fear, trouble, sickness, and sin was overcome and defeated by the work of Jesus Christ on Calvary.

The footprint of Jesus Christ is already on the neck of every fear. It cannot defeat you unless you consent to it. Throw your will on the victory side. Consent to be delivered and you will know you are more than conqueror through Jesus Christ our Lord.

After you have named your enemy and, in faith, realized your victory through Jesus Christ, get alone with God and open up your life to Him. Ask Him for a deep cleansing by the precious blood of Christ. Ask for a cleansing of your innermost being. Ask Him to wash away every hidden fear and anxiety. Allow Him to come in and fill your whole being. Let go and let God!

As His cleansing stream pours through you, the Holy Spirit will convict you of other hidden faults. As He does, confess everything He reveals, every sin, every fault, and every failure. Let the cleansing power of the blood carry it all away.

Stay before God, wait upon Him. Let Him renew you. Let God replace the driving energy of fear and worry with the true energy of faith. Then rise to your feet and in quietness and confidence serve Him.

> But whoso hearkeneth unto me shall dwell safely, and shall be quiet from fear of evil.
>
> Proverbs 1:33

8

Resentment

Many forms of spiritual illness stem from resentment. It is the *number one* offender in the lives of millions of people who are bound by its chains. From what I have gathered through reading and research, nothing can cause emotional upsets as quickly and effectively as resentment.

Why is this so? What happens to us when we become resentful? When we experience resentment, we get "ticked off" at someone because he or she hurt or threatened us in some way. We regard certain areas of our life very highly—our self-esteem, our ambitions, our security, even our personal and sex relations—and when someone dares to invade any one of these areas, we become intensely indignant and begin to wallow in self-pity.

So many people are resentful because of their lot in life, a thing over which they have no control, and yet they permit bitterness to take over. They seem to be forever bucking the tide and never getting anywhere and in so doing, they become all tied up in knots. They feel as though they are being robbed and denied the best in life. Some feel they have made a big mistake in their selection of a marriage partner and are so steeped in feeling sorry for themselves that they have become bound by resentment. Still others have met great disappointments in life and feel trapped by unalterable circumstances. So they turn against everyone, allowing themselves to become resentful even toward those who would do them good.

There are very many who have fallen into the trap of resentment over a supposed insult, some small indignity, some slight wrong, or a lack of appreciation or recognition. They pout, sulk, and before long, they are feeling sorry for themselves, held in the bondage of resentment. In self-pity they say, "Nobody loves or cares for me anymore." Resentment toward their family grows and soon the home is the scene of a cold war.

Resentment is a reaction which can creep in easily when you feel someone is taking advantage of you or willfully trespassing against you. Often you catch yourself saying of such people, "They make me sick." And that is exactly what happens. Resentment *can* make you sick just as it has made multitudes sick during the ages.

The problem of resentment is not especially peculiar to our age. It has been a large emotional boulder in man's path for centuries. Back in the days of Jesus, He saw what resentment did to people. He knew it for what it really was and so the Son of God spent considerable time teaching and warning against it.

Justifying Your Resentment   Some people maintain they have a right to be resentful. "I have been wronged. I have a right to feel this way." Friend, it is not a question of whether or not you are justified in being resentful. The fact remains that resentments are poison to body, soul, and spirit. Who wants the right to become enslaved?

In all probability, your resentments are not at all justified. Perhaps you think they are but if you examine yourself carefully, you will probably discover that your resentments are rooted in self-pity. God graciously forgave you, without reservations, when you had sinned against Him. Now you must learn to do the same. Forgive the other fellow! Hold no feelings against him regardless of where the blame belongs.

One of the most important truths I have learned in my Christian walk is this: Do not let the actions and attitudes of others determine your conduct and attitudes. If you do not adopt this rule, you will become frustrated in trying to change every person you meet. This is what Jesus taught His disciples when He sent them out to minister:

> Then he called his twelve disciples together, and gave them power and authority over all devils, and to cure diseases. And he sent them to preach the kingdom of God, and to heal the sick. And he said unto them, Take nothing for your journey, neither staves, nor scrip, neither bread, neither money; neither have two coats apiece. And whatsoever house ye enter into, there abide, and thence depart. And whosoever will not receive you, when ye go out of that city, shake off the very dust from your feet for a testimony against them.
>
> Luke 9:1–5

In other words, don't stay where you become angry and resentful. *Shake off the dust.* This is a good rule to live by. Shake off the dust before it gets into you. Don't allow the dust to linger.

So many people come away from a problem with only a partial victory simply because they allow some of the dust of resentment, some of the inward hurt or anger, to cling to them. This spoils the complete victory. There must be complete forgiveness with no strings attached or else there is no complete victory. Martin Luther once said, "My soul is too glad and too great to be the enemy of any man."

Since God forgives you, you can forgive others. If you shut up mercy from others, you shut up God's mercy toward you. Not one of us is perfect and before I die, I know I will do some wrong for which I will need forgiveness. Therefore, I cannot afford to cut myself off from God's forgiveness by not forgiving my brother—and neither can you!

Forgiveness Overcomes Resentment   Jesus said, "Take heed to yourselves! Don't let yourselves be caught in this evil web. Be careful of your reaction when a man deliberately does evil against you" (*see* Luke 17:3). A life that consists of deep resentment is a life full of futility and unhappiness. It is a grave situation, so don't harbor your hurt. Tell the man his fault. If he repents and says he is sorry, forgive him! By forgiving others, you, too, are released.

Don't hold a grudge. Don't become resentful and even if the man has done a thing deliberately seven times in one day, if he repents, you must forgive him. Let me say it again, *you must forgive him!* Why is it so important to be quick to forgive? Because if you don't forgive, you, yourself, will suffer in more ways than one. Your unforgiveness will not harm the other person—it will harm *you.* By harboring feelings of resentment, you shut yourself off from the power and direction of the Holy Spirit.

When you are unforgiving, it is because you have resented an action against you. If you refuse to forgive—by harboring resentment—a root of bitterness will develop which will grow into a massive tree. This, you will find very difficult to cut down if it is allowed to grow.

By harboring bitterness and resentment, you allow the enemy of your soul to find a dwelling place in your spirit. You cannot keep resentment in your spirit without bearing the results of it in your soul and body. When once the spirit of resentment has a foothold, you are in trouble. This spiritual problem develops into a physical problem and eventually the physical problem becomes the problem of the soul.

When you are bitter in your soul, you become resentful of everything and everybody. A vicious cycle begins which will include the entire being—spirit, soul, and body. This, my friend, is real bondage and bondage brings torment!

Peter had asked Jesus a question about forgiveness:

> . . . Lord, how oft shall my brother sin against me, and I forgive him? till seven times? Jesus saith unto him, I say not unto thee, Until seven times: but, Until seventy times seven.
>
> Matthew 18:21, 22

From this point, Jesus enlarged upon what He said by telling a parable concerning a king and one of his servants (*see* vs. 23–35).

On a certain day, the king demanded an accounting of all that was owed to him. One of his servants, who owed him ten thousand talents, had no money to pay the debt. In order that payment might be made, the king commanded that the servant, his wife, and children be sold along with all their possessions.

The servant fell down before the king and prayed for patience and forgiveness. The king relented. He had compassion upon him. The man was set free and forgiven the whole debt.

The same servant who had been forgiven this great debt had a fellow worker who owed him a hundred pence. When he found his friend who owed him the paltry sum, he took him by the throat and demanded immediate payment. Finally, when he took his hands from the fellow's throat, his friend fell down at his feet and begged for time and mercy but the servant would not listen to the man's pleas and had him thrown into prison.

When the king heard what had happened, he took this wicked, resentful servant and delivered him to the tormentors! I believe this word *tormentors* has special significance—for the result of resentment is always torment! Resentment is a horrible prison. It robs a man of all peace of mind, self-respect, and even his health. Every attempt at revenge leaves a man more frustrated, cheated, and tormented. You are being deceived if you feel you are punishing an enemy by being resentful toward him. Actually, you are selling yourself down the river into a tragic bondage.

Resentment Causes Illness I have read about experiments which showed that when anger and resentment were present in a person, the process of digestion stopped. In a group of mucous-colitis cases, 85 percent of the patients confessed they harbored resentments—against employers, parents, and life in general. All of this can be avoided by the simple act of forgiveness and a refusal to hold resentment in the heart.

In spite of all of these ill effects caused by resentment, the worst result of being resentful and unforgiving is that these feelings close the heavens above our heads! Our way into God is closed!

> Be ye therefore merciful, as your Father also is merciful. Judge not, and ye shall not be judged: condemn not, and ye shall not be condemned: forgive and ye shall be forgiven.
>
> Luke 6:36, 37

> And when ye stand praying, forgive, if ye have ought against any: that your Father also which is in heaven may forgive you your trespasses. But if ye do not forgive, neither will your Father which is in heaven forgive your trespasses.
>
> Mark 11:25, 26

This is the reason so many people have lost their way spiritually and cannot find healing for their sick bodies. Resentment and an unforgiving spirit closed the heavens above them. God cannot deliver them until they are willing to forgive others.

A Floating Emotion   A good illustration of the misery suffered because of an unforgiving spirit is that of a very unhappy woman who came to see me. She was in her early thirties, single, too heavy, and seriously down on herself. Her opening remarks were: "I never want to see my mother again. I mean it. If she comes near me, I don't know what I'll do. I will not be responsible."

I watched this young woman carefully while she spoke of her mother. She began to perspire. She stood and took off a sweater. A few minutes later, she asked if we had air conditioning. As she paced the floor, she continued her story.

"From the time I was a little girl, I was told I was fat, ugly, and would be nothing but a burden to my mother for the rest of her life. I was unwanted. I didn't seem to be the kind of child my mother had in mind. You might say I was a total disappointment. There wasn't much I could do right except eat and eventually food became my world. The more I ate, the more she complained. The more she complained, the more I ate. In time, I came to resent her with a passion!"

When she finished this statement, she was ready to leave. She became so irritated in talking about her mother that she could not go on. Finally, I got her calmed down enough to talk and asked her about the people who comprised her social circle. Her reply was, "None of them will mind their own business. They are forever telling me what I ought to do. Why don't I take off some weight? Why don't I get a better job? They are driving me up a wall."

In our sessions together, I was eventually able to show her what resentment had done and was still doing to her. She began to take notice. Resentment is a floating emotion and will not stick on the one person we initially resented—in this case, the young lady's mother. It floats and attaches itself to all our friends until we resent anyone who attempts to give us even one piece of good advice. This is precisely what happened in this case.

This woman wrestled with her resentment for weeks before she was willing to call it by its rightful name and surrender it. Even while she was surrendering it into the hands of the Lord, she was fighting to keep it. Gradually, the resentment began to wane—to a point. Months have passed and some of it still lin-

59

gers. Enough has been washed away to permit a meeting with her mother without a blowup on either side.

Her social relationships are much improved but they, too, could be much better if she could release the entire resentment. It was so deeply rooted that it is taking more time. The reason—the Lord will only wash out and away that which we want out. If we will face up to what really ails us, He will do inner and real miracles. Believe me, He will!

The True Grace of God   There are many people who cannot forgive and forget because they themselves have never really experienced the true grace of God in their own lives. The true grace of God leads a man to salvation. It is a genuine work of the Holy Spirit and when the Holy Spirit begins His work of grace, He convicts and convinces a man of all sin. Anyone who is guilty of unforgiveness or resentment has not experienced the true grace of God at work in his life.

If you have never been convicted or convinced that you are a sinner, dead in trespasses and sins, then you have never tasted the grace of God. If you feel you have never sinned, then you have never seen sin as it really is. However, when you see sin as sin, it becomes exceedingly distasteful and you run to Jesus Christ for cleansing.

When you are forgiven of your sins and know what it means to be forgiven, you will not find it difficult to forgive others in the same way you have been forgiven. You will avoid retaliation or argument. You will put out of your mind the wrongs that others have done and will begin to look for your own mistakes.

Where have you been selfish, dishonest, self-seeking, or frightened? Though a situation was not entirely your fault, did you try to disregard entirely the other person involved? Where were you to blame? Did you bother to admit your mistake honestly? Are you willing to set matters straight?

The debt which God forgives us is such a gigantic debt that it could have resulted in the very destruction of our soul. Why then should it be so difficult for us to forgive a slight, an insult, or a wrong? If we cannot find it in our hearts to forgive others, then God cannot forgive us. An unforgiving spirit reaps unforgiveness. Resentment is as sand in the machinery of heaven.

The extension of grace comes to a standstill. These resentments are not worth the loss of an access to God.

> And be ye kind to one another, tenderhearted, forgiving one another, even as God for Christ's sake hath forgiven you.
>
> Ephesians 4:32

It is impossible to hold both Christ and resentments at the same time. One or the other must go. Do you want to go through life gnawing away on resentments, a bitter, mean, calloused, and poisoned person? This will be your lot if you allow resentment to remain and grow in you.

9
Indecision

Nothing saps our strength and energy more than the agonies of indecision. We run into arguments for and against and the more we try to resolve them, the more they seem to offset each other.

This produces conflict; conflict causes breakdown; and all this ends in frustration. Perhaps you have never realized that indecision is a bondage that borders on unbelief and it can keep you from receiving anything from the hand of God. Consider the words of James on this subject:

> If any of you lack wisdom, let him ask of God, that giveth to all men liberally, and upbraideth not; and it shall be given him. But let him ask in faith, nothing wavering. For he that wavereth is like a wave of the sea driven with the wind and tossed. For let not that

man think that he shall receive anything of the Lord. A double minded man is unstable in all his ways.

James 1:5–8

Think this over carefully: A double-minded man is unstable in all his ways. When he prays, his mind fluctuates between hope and fear, between doubt and desire. His entire behavior is fickle and inconsistent. Is it any wonder that such prayer receives nothing from God?

Jesus said: ". . . No man, having put his hand to the plough, and looking back, is fit for the kingdom of God" (Luke 9:62). Those of us who want to follow Jesus must tread down all obstacles. Just as it is impossible to plow a straight furrow unless the eyes are fixed steadfastly on the mark set up by the plowman, it is impossible for us to serve God unless we keep our eyes fixed on Jesus. There is no room in the Kingdom of God for indecision!

The Valley of Indecision   There are many so-called Christians who have pitched their tents in the valley of indecision. They have not yet made up their minds that the way of Christ is the answer. Instead, they are continually looking around, considering and weighing everything that comes along. They are always wondering about things and never sure of anything. They wonder why their lives are so ineffective! It isn't hard to understand why there is no progress in their lives. They are trying to go two ways at one time. They want to live in Christ and they want to live in the world.

These people haven't decided whom they will serve. They deceive themselves by thinking they are playing a safe game. It simply cannot be done. Read these Scripture verses carefully:

Therewith bless we God, even the Father, and therewith curse we men, which are made after the similitude of God. Out of the same mouth proceedeth blessing and cursing. My brethren, these things ought not so to be. Doth a fountain send forth at the same place sweet water and bitter? Can the fig tree, my brethren, bear olive berries? either a vine, figs? So can no fountain both yield salt water and fresh.

James 3:9–12

Here we further show our inconsistency by first using the tongue to praise God and then we turn upon our fellowman with cursing and slander. In order for us to walk in right relationship with God, we must be consistent in all things. There is absolutely no other way to walk in light except our eye be on one sure goal.

Can you imagine a person spending twenty years agonizing over making a decision? This is precisely what is happening to an acquaintance of mine.

Some twenty years ago, he said, "I have a call into the ministry, I just know I have. One of these days I am going to leave my job and strike out in faith. Performing the will of God is my delight and desire." Since that time, this man has been moving from one section of the country to another and changing jobs one after another. In each city he will join a church and work for a while, but since it is not a full-time ministry, he will not stay at it.

His family suffers. They have no real and continuous friendships and are always up in the air about Daddy. They live under the assumption that one day Daddy is going into the ministry and they dare not settle down because it might not be the will of God.

This man's indecision is based upon what day he should make the break from secular work into his so-called ministry. He will never make this decision because he has the mistaken notion that the ministry is some form of degradation—it is something less than what he is presently doing. He does not feel he would be leaving his present position for something better. Instinctively, he feels he would be making a bad decision and so he makes no decision at all.

He is attempting to appease God who he feels has called him and it seems better to delay this decision than to simply say that he has no intention of answering the call into the ministry. This man is making himself unfit for the Kingdom of God, but continues to keep his hand on the plow even though he doesn't know which way to turn.

One Certain Direction   Because of indecision, there are multitudes in the same wretched state as this man. They are like the man in the Bible who was possessed with legions of devils, each one of them demanding that the man do his particular bidding. It is no small wonder that the man was a lunatic.

Indecision and double-mindedness can pull and tear people in a dozen different directions at once. Such people are in bondage just as surely as the man who was bound by many devils. There is no worse bondage than to have a legion of devils within, each trying to dominate the victim and drag him in a particular direction.

Millions of miserable people would find deliverance today if they would cast their vote for God, get their eyes upon Him and head in one certain direction. This is the only certain direction! This is what repentance is. It is the God-given realization that your present direction is dead wrong and you decide to turn around. You give yourself to Christ that He might direct your life and enter into a new life of peace, rest, and confidence in Him. If you have been in the bondage of indecision and double-mindedness, you must decide the course you will pursue and then give yourself wholeheartedly to it.

If you decide to follow Jesus Christ, you must determine to make up your mind that you will follow Him, come what may. You have to be completely sold out on Jesus! Anytime you say, "I'll think it over," you can rest assured it's only a cop-out—a feeble excuse to avoid making a decision. What is there to think about? If you are acquainted with the facts of a situation, the answer is usually quite apparent. If you decide to follow Christ, you submit yourself to Him completely and with no reservations.

It is important to grasp the fact that God's way is the best and only way. Don't have the mistaken notion that there might be something better somewhere else and shop around before making a commitment. Sheer nonsense! Any direction we go with Christ is a sure road; any other direction is toward bondage.

Many of our young people have adopted the foolish idea that going the way of Christ is bondage. They have put their hands to the plow but they are looking all around, standing still, and not going anywhere. Flirting with the world and yielding to the things which attract them is making them double-minded and unfit for God's Kingdom.

Being deceived into thinking that these other things are liberties, these young people are becoming ensnared like a fly in a spider's web. The Word of God is not binding—it is a light and lamp which guides a young man's feet away from bondage! Jesus Christ didn't come to circumscribe anyone. He came that we might have life and have it more abundantly. We have been hoodwinked into thinking that there can be other ways to happiness outside of Christ, but this is not true. God knew what He was saying when He inspired Paul to write:

> Be ye not unequally yoked together with unbelievers: for what fellowship hath righteousness with unrighteousness? and what communion hath light with darkness? And what concord hath Christ with Belial? or what part hath he that believeth with an infidel? And what agreement hath the temple of God with idols? for ye are the temple of the living God; as God hath said, I will dwell in them, and walk in them; and I will be their God, and they shall be my people.

> 2 Corinthians 6:14–16

You who are trying to go in two directions at the same time, let me ask you a few questions. Just what fellowship has righteousness with unrighteousness? What do you have in common as a basis of communication? What realm of agreement do you have? What agreement has one whose body has become the temple of the living God with one who is unclean, and walks in sin and filth? Let me answer this for you—absolutely none!

If you are living as a true Christian believer, you wouldn't even consider entering into any kind of relationship (whether it be business or personal) with unbelievers. As a true believer, you cannot share in that which appeals to unbelievers. Complete union with God involves a complete separation from the world.

Indecision Causes Bondage   Some of you will say, "I know what you say is true but I just can't seem to be able to stand up and say *yes* or *no* when I should give a definite answer." This is something no one can do for you. Only you have the power to make yourself say no or yes. If you don't make up your mind, indecision will bring you into a bondage of frustration and turmoil.

Let us examine a few facts. As a human being, you must make your own decisions. You cannot go through life having someone else deciding for you, nor can you go through life avoiding decisions and all unpleasant situations. You are continually faced with the problem of making decisions.

These times come to every man. To avoid making a decision simply because you don't want to make a wrong one leaves you in the place of indecision. Many times, when you have spent hours, days, or weeks painfully thinking out a decision and then the decision you did make turns out to be wrong, inevitably you can go back and see that your original hunch would have been the right move for you to make.

I have found that the best way to make a decision is not according to what I would like but on the basis of right principles. When I am faced with a problem, I consider the right and wrong of it and then base my decision on the right principle regardless of how I am affected.

When faced with serious, momentous decisions, pray! Ask God for direction, expect to receive it, and when you do, follow it! Our God will guide those who seek His direction if it is sought in honesty and sincerity. He will not fail!

Many Voices   In moments of indecision, many people make the sad mistake of asking for much counsel from others. This is foolhardy, to say the least. When you ask a multitude of people for counsel, you receive a multitude of words and ideas. The result is greater conflict and indecision than before. If you cannot get an answer from God by yourself, then seek out a person who truly knows God and ask that friend for advice. Then act upon it.

There is a very necessary truth we must all learn—after you have decided, let your decision stand. Do not waver. Don't allow double-mindedness to creep in. I have counseled with many people over the years. Some come back to me after making a decision, in conflict, wondering if they had made the right decision. Never let yourself be torn like this. When once you have decided a thing, let your decision remain and don't mull it over.

Every decision we make is not always the right decision. If you make a wrong decision and it happens in sincerity of heart, God can and will overrule. Our God can still make all things work together for good to them who love Him, who are the called according to His purpose (*see* Romans 8:28).

One great truth from which we reap much comfort is the knowledge that God forgives and forgets the past failures of the person who walks with Him. If we can forgive ourselves for our past mistakes and get a new and certain direction in our lives, we too can forget the past and live a very happy life.

Paul's Mistakes   The Apostle Paul made some very erroneous decisions in his lifetime but he learned to put the past behind him and press toward his new goal. He had been very sure that the followers of Jesus Christ were wrong. He was sure they were a deluded people who had to be stopped in their heresy and he went to great lengths to carry out his convictions. He persecuted the disciples of Jesus with great vehemence.

The day Paul was stopped by Christ, he came to the shocking realization that his convictions about the Christians were wrong. These people were right and he was wrong! Paul was quick to make an about-face. He confessed the errors of his past, decided to live for Christ and left his former life behind. In this way, his conscience was purged by the blood of Christ, letting him forget his past. This experience was so real to Paul that he wrote about it to the Philippian church:

> Brethren, I count not myself to have apprehended: but this one thing I do, forgetting those things which are

behind, and reaching forth unto those things which are before, I press toward the mark for the prize of the high calling of God in Christ Jesus.

Philippians 3:13, 14

Paul told this church the same thing Christ told His disciples. Forget all the sins and shortcomings, aims and ambitions of the past that they may not be a hindrance to you in your race to your goal—complete conformity to Jesus in His glory. Put your hand to the plow and keep on plowing! Head for the prize! Don't let yourself be hindered. Don't look around and allow yourself to lose your sense of direction. Keep your eye on the goal!

If you find yourself hopelessly in bondage to the sin of double-mindedness and indecision, make your way to the Lord. In the Name of Jesus Christ, He will break the bands and fetters that bind you. You can be set free to go on your way rejoicing. When faced with a decision, remember that those who get things done are the spontaneous people who respond to life's situations without hesitation.

10
Jealousy

"My husband is driving me up the wall. I can't go shopping alone or even visit the next-door neighbor without being accused of having an affair with every man who walks down the street. I think he's going out of his mind."

I said, "Come on now, you are exaggerating."

The woman to whom I was speaking was in her late fifties. She and her husband had been married for just a few months, each for the second time. She was a widow; he, a widower.

"I'm not exaggerating," she said. "You can call him in and ask him for yourself. He's out there waiting for me now."

I called him in. He came into the study and sat down sheepishly. I confronted him with the problem by saying, "Your wife tells me you won't allow her out of your sight and are accusing her of unfaithfulness. Is this the truth?"

"Brother Jim, it is. As you can see, my wife is a beautiful woman and I'm not sure just how or why she consented to be my wife. I watch the faces of men. They are after her, believe me."

I could hardly believe my ears. His wife was a nice average woman, but certainly no raving beauty. I knew she was a woman of character who could be trusted and who had no weaknesses where men were concerned. What the man was saying was simply not true and time proved that it was not true. Jealousy had completely distorted the picture and was about to ruin this marriage.

In dealing with the man, I was able to show him that the problem was not with his wife, but with him, and unless this jealousy was washed out by the power of the Holy Spirit, he would ruin any meaningful relationship he would ever enter into.

Gradually, he saw jealousy for what it really was and opened his life to the deep washing of the Holy Spirit. The areas of distrust that lay deep in his subconscious mind began to flow away. The man was set free. His marriage was saved.

Jealousy Breeds Violence   Jealous people are domineering, possessive, grudging, envious, and suspicious. They have a rather naive notion that whatever they want should be theirs for the asking with little concern for the opinions or feelings of others. This not only brings torment and unhappiness to them but it affects everyone with whom they have daily contact.

They are self-centered and demanding individuals. Everything must go their way! And when it doesn't, their frustration erupts in anger and false accusations. Most of the time, the very thing they accuse the other person of doing is what they would like to be doing themselves. The man who accuses his wife of unfaithfulness may actually be the unfaithful party. In his subconscious mind, if he is not overtly unfaithful, you can be sure he would like to be!

Jealous people lust and, because they cannot possess, they become harsh and empty. When their demands are not met, they become sullen, cruel, and often violent. The spirit of jealousy can become so strong that it can drive a person to murder, as in the case of Cain and Abel:

> But unto Cain and to his offering he [God] had not respect. And Cain was very wroth, and his countenance fell. And the Lord said unto Cain, Why art thou wroth? and why is thy countenance fallen? If thou doest well, shalt thou not be accepted? and if thou doest not well, sin lieth at the door. And unto thee shall be his desire, and thou shalt rule over him. And Cain talked with Abel his brother: and it came to pass, when they were in the field, that Cain rose up against Abel his brother, and slew him.
>
> Genesis 4:5–8

Cain killed his brother because his own works were wicked, while his brother's were just. He was resentfully envious of Abel. There is a lesson for us to learn here—one sin not repented prepares the way for other and greater sins. Cain's jealousy led to murder which he attempted to cover up by lying to God. God condemns violent reactions of rage against others, as we see by His severe punishment of Cain:

> And now art thou cursed from the earth, which hath opened her mouth to receive thy brother's blood from thy hand; When thou tillest the ground, it shall not henceforth yield unto thee her strength; a fugitive and a vagabond shalt thou be in the earth.
>
> Genesis 4:11, 12

When sin is not confessed, but excused, we open the door to bondage. Sin against God or our fellowman is always accompanied by guilt which puts a limitation upon our lives. When we observe others who are without that limitation, jealousy is exercised by striking out against them in strife and envy. Before long, this attitude warps our entire personality. An inner spiritual war is begun.

Release Through Christ   I have seen homes on the brink of collapse because of a jealous spirit which caused unbearable heartache and misery. I have also seen the intervening hand of God lay an axe to the root of that bondage and set that home free.

A woman and her husband were at the point of divorce when she came to see me. She was going to divorce him because he did not love her anymore—in fact, the husband seemed to prefer their daughter.

"You should see the way he fawns over that girl," she told me. "He gives her anything she wants because she has him wrapped around her finger. What she needs is a good *pop* right where it would do the most good!"

Our interview didn't continue long before it became apparent that the problem was with the mother and the daughter competing for the affections of the husband and father. Her story went this way: "Before the birth of my daughter, my husband and I were lovers but after she was born, everything changed." The word *she* came out of her mouth through clenched teeth.

"When he would come home from work, he would go right to that crib. Most of the evening was spent with her. He didn't seem to have time for me anymore and I still don't understand why." As she spoke, she picked up her purse and extracted a wallet, then handed me a picture of her daughter—a girl about fifteen years of age and quite pretty.

"Look at her. The girl's eyes are too close together and that mouth is too large to be beautiful." She tore the girl apart.

I suggested to her that her dominant emotion was jealousy. "Jealous of her? Are you kidding?" When she saw I wasn't kidding and meant business, she broke down and cried.

Instant confession followed as she said, "I just had to talk to someone. I know I am jealous of my own daughter and it's causing me to make life a hell for everyone. I must get it out of me."

We faced this jealousy head-on. When she had confessed that she had become a jealous woman, she realized that she needed to be changed and only Christ could do that. She surrendered herself into the hands of Jesus and asked for an inner washing and cleansing through His precious blood. It happened.

She went into the waters of baptism to bury the woman she used to be. Following her baptism, she began to walk in newness of life, a new creature in Christ Jesus, a new mother, a new wife and, consequently, she began living in a new and different home environment.

Thank God, there is a way of release through Jesus Christ our Lord! The way out of all guilt and self-condemnation is through Jesus Christ, the Son of God. Always remember, God loves you. He always has.

> For God so loved the world, that he gave his only begotten Son, that whosoever believeth in Him, should not perish, but have everlasting life.
>
> John 3:16

Because God loves you, He wants you to live in righteousness, joy, and peace in the Holy Spirit and He will release you if you come to Him. Look at it this way. If God didn't spare His own Son that He might bring us salvation and release from the guilt of sin, then why hold on to sin and let it ruin your life?

No Immunity Jealous people are like a tornado roaring its way through the lives of others. No one is immune to jealousy. There are times when we all experience its devastating effects. The apostles of Jesus were not immune to it. It manifested itself through John and James when they selfishly insisted that Jesus allow them to sit on the thrones next to His in the Kingdom—they boldly asked Jesus for this honor:

And James and John, the sons of Zebedee, come unto him, saying, Master, we would that thou shouldest do for us whatsoever we shall desire. And he said unto them, What would ye that I should do for you? They said unto him, Grant unto us that we may sit, one on thy right hand, and the other on thy left hand, in thy glory.

Mark 10:35–37

In those days, the two places of greatest honor in a monarchy were considered to be the right and left side of the reigning king. Little did the two apostles know the kind of kingdom they were about to enter! They probably saw themselves as ruling despots of some oriental kingdom in which their whims and desires would be the only law.

John evidently was not the meek, mild, and amiable person we picture him to be, for Jesus saw the fiery dispositions of both James and John and called them "the sons of thunder" (*see* Mark 3:17). He knew what was in their hearts and He knew how to handle them. Their request was so terribly atrocious that the other ten apostles became highly indignant.

Calmly, Jesus explained to all of them that the degree of their greatness and sovereignty would depend on two things: (1) to be great, they had to become as servants; (2) to be first in the Kingdom, they had to become slaves (*see* Mark 10:42–45). In other words, their degree of unselfishness would be the determining factor of their status in the Kingdom. By learning to serve everybody, from the lowest to the highest, the urge for greatness would be eliminated and the possibility of jealousy would diminish.

The Prodigal Son   My mind is drawn to the story of the Prodigal Son (*see* Luke 15:11–32). This young man, the younger son in the family, came one day and asked his father for the inheritance which was rightfully his. The father gave it to him and the son left home. The fellow was not at all wise. He joined himself to a stranger of a far country. Eventually, his inheritance was all spent on a way of life that produced only evil.

73

When he came to his senses, he found himself wallowing in a pigpen! He was down on the level of the swine!

When he had had enough, he said to himself, "I'm getting out of here. I will go back to my father and ask him to let me have a servant's place. His servants are far better off than I am. I know I have sinned against my father and against God but I will ask for mercy."

When the father saw him coming, he said to his servants, "Get out the best robe and put it on him. Get a ring for his finger and shoes for his feet. Kill the fatted calf. Let's have a feast. This, my son, was dead but now he is alive again."

The errant son had committed some terrible wrongs, but he came home repentant of his past. Now the elder brother who had never left home reacted to this scene of forgiveness with hardness of heart, unforgiveness, and resentment. He could not bless his brother nor could he rejoice with the father. The parable ends with the younger brother in the father's house and the elder brother on the outside looking in, seething in jealousy and all that goes with it.

Negative Christians   The church today is filled with people who pride themselves on the fact that they do not steal, lie, get drunk, or commit adultery. Yet, these same people do not bless or rejoice when a sinner comes in and is forgiven.

They judge the man because of his past and they will not forget it. They are jealous, resentful, and angry that such a one should be accepted into the church and considered on an equal status with them. Eventually, because of this, they end up on the outside of the door with all the rest of the unrepentant!

Jealousy spoils everything it comes in contact with. It takes beautiful situations and turns them into something vile and offensive; it takes beautiful people and makes them repulsive individuals; it kills love and makes friendships impossible.

Overcoming Jealousy   What can we do when jealousy begins to destroy us and our relationships with others? Fighting it will only drive it deep into the subconscious where it will lie dormant for a time, only to erupt later. The answer is to recognize that jealousy is like a malignancy that must be cut out—

roots and all—or it will continue to grow.

To root it out completely, accept the fact that jealousy gets you absolutely nowhere with the person you love. It is difficult to love a person who is suspicious, envious, and selfish. If you are a jealous person, you are a selfish, self-centered individual. Bring your jealousy out into the open and surrender it to God, along with all the negative emotions that go with it. Then begin to see the good in the person who is the object of your jealousy. Pray for that person and before long, your attitude will begin to change.

The wonder of the love of God is that God loves the sinner and hates the sin. This is the mystery of godliness. God loves the sinner but He hates the sin that has him enslaved. By the love of God that has been shed abroad in our souls, we are able to do the same. Learn to love yourself and your own soul—which has great value—and work to save your soul. As you learn to do so, you will begin to hate the sin and the bondage which has your soul bound.

Remember that no one ever treated you any worse than you have treated God. Yet—He forgave you and forgot! Now God isn't asking you to do anything that He Himself does not do, and He will supply you with what it takes to do it!

11

Uncleanness

Uncleanness has taken hold of so many in our generation that we could well be the wicked generation of which Jesus Christ spoke. We can be unclean by indulging in the sins of uncleanness and lust, but the Bible clearly teaches that there is a bondage of uncleanness which is brought about by an unclean spirit. Here are some biblical examples of this truth:
Christ Himself cast out unclean spirits:

75

And they were all amazed, insomuch that they questioned among themselves, saying, What thing is this? what new doctrine is this? for with authority commandeth he even the unclean spirits, and they do obey him.

Mark 1:27

Christ gave His disciples power to cast out unclean spirits:

And when he had called unto him his twelve disciples, he gave them power against unclean spirits, to cast them out, and to heal all manner of sickness and all manner of disease.

Matthew 10:1

After the church was born on the day of Pentecost, it continued in this same vein of ministry in power and authority:

Insomuch that they brought forth the sick unto the streets, and laid them on beds and couches, that at least the shadow of Peter passing by might overshadow some of them. There came also a multitude out of the cities round about unto Jerusalem, bringing sick folks, and them which were vexed with unclean spirits: and they were healed every one.

Acts 5:15, 16

This same power to minister was also given to the church evangelists as illustrated in the ministry of Philip:

And the people with one accord gave heed unto those things which Philip spake, hearing and seeing the miracles which he did. For unclean spirits, crying with loud voice, came out of many that were possessed with them: and many taken with palsies, and that were lame, were healed.

Acts 8:6, 7

According to the Bible record, we can conclude without a doubt that there is such a thing or power as an unclean spirit. It is clear from these Scripture verses that this type of bondage brings sickness, infirmity, heartache, and trouble. Where does this kind of bondage have its beginning?

The Power of Sex   There is little doubt that one of the greatest drives and powers in humanity is the power of sex. In many instances, the bondage of uncleanness has its beginning with a wrong attitude toward sex. Many people believe and teach that only instinct should govern this God-given power. Let us examine this theory and see how wrong it is and where it leads.

Instinct is the animal level of life. Man was not meant to live on this level. Yet, considering the use of sex on the animal level, we find it is not without inhibition. It is governed and regulated by the mating season and the cycle of procreation. Nature imposes its own restrictions and the animal world is subject to them.

There are some people who defy even the dictates of nature. They want to live without inhibitions or restrictions of any kind whether they be natural, social, or moral. In their pursuit of this so-called freedom, they don't realize that they are courting disaster which will be their ruination.

In dealing with man, we are not dealing with an animal. No matter what anthropologists or sociologists tell us, man is on a higher level than animals. It is little wonder we have the problems of today when we consider the things our children are being taught in our present-day school systems. By and large, our boys and girls are being taught that man is the most intelligent animal on earth. If this were true, then man could live in the realm of instinct and have no condemnation or repercussions. We know this is not true. Man's level of life is in the realm of moral law. Animals survive as they respond to their physical environment and, when this is no longer possible, they die. On the level of man, the secret of survival is more than a response to physical environment.

The moral environment to which man is expected to respond has not been set up by man in the form of codes of conduct; it

77

is built into the very nature of man by God Himself. Break these laws, and you will be broken! Restraints are placed on the pursuit of instinct by this built-in moral law. Either you find them and use them in their God-appointed time and place or you lose their blessing and they become a curse to you.

Sex Fulfilled   The God-appointed time and place for sex is in marriage—one man and one woman living together in moral faithfulness. A home is established, love is the bond, and children are born. This is the fulfillment of sex—beautiful and wonderful—without bondage.

If you believe the lie that you can have sex apart from God's laws, apart from morality, you will eventually and without exception end up in the bondage of uncleanness. You will not have sex—sex will have you. It will rule your thinking, your actions, and finally your whole life. You will become its slave. This is bondage!

This is what is happening to this ill-advised, ill-taught, perverted, immoral generation of today. Many foolish people tell the young and the frustrated to find themselves a man or woman regardless of the consequences! They advocate unrestrained indulgence in sex as the urge demands. This is no cure for the conflict. It is like pouring gasoline on an already raging fire.

The moral laws and the Ten Commandments both say, "Thou shalt not commit adultery." If you break these laws, you begin to perish immediately. Our hospitals and institutions are filled with people who dared to break these laws. One day they awoke to find themselves skidding down the slippery road to ruin, bound in the chains of lust, burning with desire, and broken in mind and body. Man cannot live like an animal. The moral law will not let him. He must meet God's terms as God's creation or pay the cost for his disobedience. There are no two ways about it.

God's Grace   People write to me saying, "Pastor Beall, I want to do what is right in this regard but I just don't have the willpower." The person who is caught in the web of bondage to sex and is fighting it with his own willpower is bound to lose the battle. The reason? In fighting it, your attention is concentrated on it, and again the imagination is aroused!

The more you concentrate on sex, the more it preys on your mind, the more you are tempted and likely to fall. You become entangled in a warfare to pull down that evil imagination. We are told that in any battle between the imagination and the will, the imagination always wins.

The answer lies in getting your attention focused on a higher power. This is your only hope for release. You must set your thoughts and affections on things above. You must come to Jesus Christ with your problem. Only He can help you. Open your life to Him and allow the power of grace to begin its work. This is your only solution. This is your only salvation.

When you come to Christ confessing your sins and are baptized in water for the remission of sins, you become a vessel for the spirit of grace. As this spirit of grace surges through your life, it will cleanse and direct your thoughts into proper channels. You will dwell on the good things God has prepared for those who love Him.

To Be Clean   Overcoming uncleanness is not accomplished by sheer willpower or determination. It requires turning the problem over to God and being willing to let Him fight your battle for you. This is how a single man in his late twenties was able to master his problem of uncleanness.

When he came into my office, he told me, "Brother Jim, every so often, I go to the bank and draw out a sizable amount of money to spend on prostitutes. I know this is wrong but I go ahead and do it just the same. What's wrong with me? Why do you think I do it?"

I asked him, "Do you feel driven at this time? Is the compulsion so great you cannot resist it?"

His answer was, "No, I can say no if I want to, but I just don't want to."

"Then you don't consider this to be sin or wrong in the sight of God," I said to him. "God will help any man to gain power over sin if that is the desire of the man, but He will leave you on your own if you want to play with sin, and if you play with it long enough, it will become your master."

He then asked, "What do I do?"

"Put your will on the side of the will of God."

"What do you mean by that?"

"I mean this," I said. "The will of God for you, even your sanctification, is that you abstain from fornication, wrong sex, and uncleanness. You must *will* the will of God for your life. You must say as Jesus said, 'My will is to do the will of Him that sent Me.' " (*See* John 5:30.)

"You mean I must make a deliberate decision in my mind about this?"

"Exactly," I replied. "Jesus Christ will move into the life of any person who will say to Him, 'I will to be clean.' He will make the person clean who wills to be clean."

He thought for a while, then said, "I want to be done with my uncleanness. I really do. I will to be clean. Jesus, make me clean."

And Jesus said in a soft and tender voice, "I will. . . . Be clean."

The Price of Bondage   In a previous chapter, I mentioned that spiritual problems are open doors to physical problems. The words of Acts 5:16 bear this out. They tell us that many sick people and those who were tormented with unclean spirits were brought to Peter and were healed. The way they were healed is recorded for us in Mark 1:27 and Matthew 10:1. Christ, with the authority of the Holy Spirit, commanded the unclean spirits to come out and they obeyed Him. The disciples were also given power and authority to cast out unclean spirits.

Today, Christ's disciples also have the same power and authority. The Lord Jesus yet commissions men and grants them authority over demons and unclean spirits. This is a lost truth to so many because the church-general has lost the power and authority of that great commission. Jesus said at the time of His Ascension:

> . . . go ye into all the world, and preach the gospel to every creature. He that believeth and is baptized shall be saved; but he that believeth not shall be damned. And these signs shall follow them that believe; In my name shall they cast out devils; they shall speak with

new tongues; They shall take up serpents; and if they drink any deadly thing, it shall not hurt them; they shall lay hands on the sick, and they shall recover.

Mark 16:15–19

Yes, unclean spirits can be cast out today by men and women of God! After they are cast out, what happens then? Jesus said:

When the unclean spirit is gone out of a man, he [the unclean spirit] walketh through dry places, seeking rest, and findeth none. Then he saith, I will return into my house from whence I came out [Satan considers the man his property, but he is only a usurper]; and when he is come, he findeth it empty, swept, and garnished. Then goeth he, and taketh with himself seven other spirits more wicked than himself, and they enter in and dwell there: and the last state of that man is worse than the first. . . .

Matthew 12:43–45

Whenever a person is released from the power of an unclean spirit, he must fill his life with the spirit of grace or the unclean spirit will come in again. A person cannot stay empty. If he or she does not let God fill the empty place, the unclean spirit will again gain entrance and bring with him seven other spirits! They will enter in and dwell there and the last state of such a person will be much worse than the first.

The Wrong Idea   A doctor once told his patients, "Your brain is your chauffeur. If the brain gets drunk with a wrong idea, you'll land in the ditch." This is exactly what happened to a young lady who fell into uncleanness because she had the wrong idea about herself. She was going from one sexual affair to another and didn't like what was happening to her.

"I'm beginning to feel dirty, unclean. I used to feel I was doing the smart thing, having a ball, but not anymore."

The girl was down on herself and had been for a long time. As we talked, I realized that because of wrong thinking she considered herself worthless and this stemmed from the fact that she had come from a very negative home environment.

She told me, "I remember from the time I was a little girl the shame I felt for my mother. She drank a lot and would bring men to the house while my dad was away. I was just a kid but I knew something was wrong. The way they acted and talked made me feel uneasy. One day I came to know what was happening when men spent the night at our house. I was angry. I couldn't believe it. I wanted to run away and hide.

"I hated my mother for what she was doing and I hated my dad for allowing it by being away from home so much. I didn't know what to do but I determined I would never be like my mother. Yet I knew I was so much like her."

News of what was happening in the home eventually reached the neighbors who warned their children to stay away from the girl who lived in such an unclean mess.

She began to think of herself as unclean and it didn't take her long to believe it. "I came to realize at a young age that I was unclean and worthless. This is the way it was and I felt I couldn't do anything about it. So why try? Why buck the crowd? When boys wanted to date me and suggested sex to me, I said, 'Why not?' But I can't take it anymore. I heard you say on the radio that Jesus Christ can restore your self-respect and make you feel like you're worth something. Do you suppose that can happen to me?"

I was so glad I could say, "Yes, He loves you and will deal with you personally. He doesn't look at you as your mother's daughter, the child of a promiscuous woman. Christ looks at you as someone who needs His help and He is pleased to give it. Do you really want to be through with your uncleanness? If in your mind you want to change, Jesus will turn your life into something meaningful."

We got down on our knees before the Lord and she opened her life to the divine invasion of the Son of God. He came in. He washed that girl, cleansed her. She has never again been the same young lady who walked into my office that day.

Many people have the wrong idea that you can enjoy sex contrary to the will of God. If you entertain that idea, you will land in the ditch!

Wild Gourds   In the days of the Prophet Elisha, a man had shred some wild gourds into a pot of herbs. The people cried, "O man of God, there is death in the pot!" Elisha heard the cry. He threw some meal into the pot and the pottage was healed (*see* 2 Kings 4:38–41). Many have shred some pretty wild gourds into the pot of truth and it has produced death. However, there is hope. If we will take the true meal of God's Word and mix it in, the pot can yet be healed.

Don't allow the good things of God to become warped in your life. God is looking out for your best interests in life. His laws are for your good. He is the "author and finisher" of your faith (*see* Hebrews 12:2) and the Spirit of God will always lead you to heights the world cannot offer.

Everything about God is creative and full of light. Walk in His ways and you will never stumble. Obey God's laws and you will be rewarded for your choice.

12

Dishonesty

Our world is divided into two camps: that of truth and that of dishonesty. The first is of God; the second is of Satan, the father of lies. Since the axis of the world passes between these two camps, Christians must choose between the two—and one of the first requirements of the Christian life is to put aside all forms of dishonesty:

. . . . Don't just pretend to be good! Be done with dishonesty and jealousy and talking about others behind their backs. Now that you realize how good the Lord has been to you, put away all evil, deception, envy, and fraud.

1 Peter 2:1, 2 LB

As we see in these Scripture verses, dishonesty covers a broad area. It includes such sins as slander, detraction (revealing the hidden faults of someone), perjury, rash judgment, malice, deceit, hypocrisy, envy, fraud, bribery, and so on.

In dealing with dishonesty, we deal with a person's basic character. The test questions concerning a man's character are these: Will he lie? Will he be truthful under all circumstances? Is he trustworthy? Can he be trusted when no eye is upon him and he is left alone with his conscience?

If these questions cannot be answered with an unqualified *yes,* then all else is in vain—and even dangerous. It is bad enough to be dishonest in the various areas of everyday life but to be dishonest in spiritual things means real trouble, for to be dishonest with God affects the very roots of a man's personality.

The Early Church　　　　Honesty was a major factor in the early church. There was something about the atmosphere in that infant community of Christians at Jerusalem which caused deception to be exposed. In the Book of Acts we read about Ananias and his wife, Sapphira, and how Satan led them to attempt to deceive the Holy Spirit (*see* Acts 5:1–10).

They had sold some property and gave only part of the money to the apostles, claiming it was the full amount. Greed caused them to retain some of the money and vanity caused them to pretend they had given all of it. When they attempted to cover up their deception by lying, their lie was immediately exposed and they could not endure the shock of such a disclosure. We are not told exactly what happened to them but we do know the Lord God did not strike them dead—they just fell over:

> But Peter said, Ananias, why hath Satan filled thine heart to lie to the Holy Ghost, and to keep back part of the price of the land? . . . why hast thou conceived this thing in thine heart? thou hast not lied unto men, but unto God. And Ananias hearing these words fell

84

down, and gave up the ghost: and great fear came on
all them that heard these things.

Acts 5:3–5

The same thing happened to Sapphira. In lying to Peter,
Ananias and Sapphira in reality lied to the Holy Spirit. The
judgment of God was necessary in their case to show the young
Christian community the respect that is due to the Holy Spirit
and to the church, which makes up the Body of Christ.

Truth is the quality of something stable and proven, something reliable. Therefore, when we speak of a true peace, we
mean a secure, lasting peace. A true road is one that will lead
us to a determined objective. A man of truth is a man who can
be trusted and his trustworthiness elicits our confidence in him.
God is trustworthy because He is faithful in keeping His promises to us.

Because Christ Himself was "full of grace and truth," He
desires that all who name His Name speak the truth at all times.
We are not to tell half-truths or circumvent the truth. The
Apostle Paul said:

> This is the ministry which God in his mercy has given
> us and nothing can daunt us. We have set our faces
> against all shameful secret practices; we use no clever
> tricks, no dishonest manipulation of the Word of God.
> We speak the plain truth and so commend ourselves to
> every man's conscience in the sight of God.

2 Corinthians 4:1, 2 PHILLIPS

Christ was relentless in upholding truth. He did not pull
down His standards to conform to ours. We must come up to His
standards. He saves us from ourselves by hard refusals. To have
the work of the Holy Spirit continue in your life demands complete honesty. He cannot be retained without it!

Christ's Coming   When Jesus Christ came to dwell among
us in the Incarnation, He did not come to bring us a new reli-

gion or a new philosophy. He did not come to bring us a new vocabulary of religious words and phrases. He came to show us how to live in harmony with the Father and in harmony with life.

Through Jesus, God was going to show that He was concerned with people. He was going to make the bodies of men and women the temples of the Holy Spirit. The Eternal determined to live within human bodies in the person of the Holy Spirit.

God would reveal Himself to men—by men. He would show Himself through the lives of people. He was going to do this so people of the world would get a true picture of God.

People would know God in terms they could understand. They would see the power of God at work in the lives of those around them. Men would be changed. They would see the Lord God change a liar into a teller of truth. By this they would know that God deals only with the truth. God never makes a man into a liar. This would be plainly revealed.

Christ and Truth   Jesus came to show us that the Lord God was completely finished with sacred buildings and places and, in the enormity of His plan, He was vitally concerned with individuals.

The purpose of God which had been hidden from ages and generations was revealed through Christ. The Word which Christ heard from the Father is the truth which He had come to proclaim and for which He gave testimony. We read that Jesus said:

> . . . but he that sent me is true; and I speak to the world those things which I have heard of him. [Jesus further proclaims:] But now ye seek to kill me, a man that hath told you the truth, which I have heard of God. . . .

> John 8:26, 40

When Jesus was brought before Pilate, His words to Pilate were:

> . . . . Thou sayest that I am a king. To this end was I born, and for this cause came I into the world, that I

should bear witness unto the truth. Every one that is of the truth heareth my voice.

John 18:37

At a time when His life was in jeopardy, Jesus told Pilate that all who love truth are His followers. If we say we belong to God and there is no change in our inner character, we lie to ourselves. If we practice lying to ourselves, we are the worst kind of liar. We are deceived at the very core!

If our words do not correspond with our actions—if we say one thing and do another—we are a living lie. This is worse than telling a falsehood with the tongue. This is living a falsehood! Those who name the Name of Jesus Christ cannot risk such a distortion. Truth must be engraved in the inner man. Only then will all phases and expressions of life be honest.

Did Jesus Christ tell the truth about the Father? I am sure you will answer this with an emphatic *yes!* Then how or in what way did Christ tell the truth about His Father? His life demonstrated His divine qualities and attributes.

Now allow me to ask a question that concerns you. Are you a true picture of what the Lord God can do in a human life through redemption? Be truthful about it! Do your children see reflected in you a true picture of what it is to be a Christian? Or do you claim to be a Christian and reflect unchristian characteristics? Is your life a lie?

Fidelity   When we deal with honesty and dishonesty, we come face-to-face with the word *fidelity*—a word absent in many a modern vocabulary. Jesus spoke of the absolute necessity of fidelity when He said, "If you are not faithful and honest in a trifle, you cannot be trusted with the tremendous. If you are not faithful with the material, how can you be entrusted with the spiritual—true riches?" (*See* Luke:16:10, 11.)

I recall a businessman who came to me and said, "I don't know what is wrong with me and my business. I make money but I don't seem to get ahead. I seem to be putting my money into a bag with holes. What do you think could be the problem?"

"Are you tithing?" I asked. "Are you faithfully giving the

Lord the first tenth of your income as you have been taught?"

"Well, no. Business has not been what it ought to be so I have fallen a little behind this year. I'll make it up as soon as I get on top of things."

I shook him when I said, "You are becoming a dishonest person. You have made a promise to God and you know tithing is a divine principle, yet you feel the Lord should bless you over your dishonesty. He will not do it. If you are not honest in your tithe-giving before God, you will discover yourself cutting corners in business, and dishonesty will honeycomb your entire enterprise. No doubt the dishonesty is apparent in other areas of your life and business. How about it?"

His reply was, "Yes, it is the truth. I have been cutting corners and have been practicing dishonesty but I have not wanted to call it that. You have placed your finger on the cancer eating at my life and business."

Laying an axe to the root of every dishonest thing in your life is vital, as this man learned. The universe and the God who made it will not back up a lie.

What We Say　　　We must be truthful in what we are. As Christians, we must have no deceit in us. We must be truthful in what we do, what we are, and what we say. The Living Bible puts it this way:

> Stop lying to each other; tell the truth, for we are parts of each other and when we lie to each other we are hurting ourselves.
>
> Ephesians 4:25 LB

We are told that the expressions of a thing deepen the impression. In other words, to think a thing makes an impression, but to *say* the same thing deepens the impression. We actually become the incarnation of what we express in words. This is in perfect harmony with Christ's words: "For by thy words thou shalt be justified, and by thy words thou shalt be condemned" (Matthew 12:37).

I never fully understood these words until I realized that we become what we say. This line of truth has some tremendous and very serious implications. It makes us know that there is no such thing as a white lie. Every so-called white lie leaves a black mark upon the soul—upon the personality.

Silence Is Golden In the silence of your mind, perhaps you are asking the question, "Are there not occasions in every life when a lie is justifiable?" No, absolutely not! Evil produces its own kind—more evil. Evil means always produce evil ends. Lies cannot bring forth good.

It is vital for every Christian to learn to discipline his tongue. Lying only shows disagreement between thought and tongue and there are times and occasions in life when we should say nothing. We must learn to bridle our tongues. We need not express an opinion about everything! Not one of us is the personification of wisdom. Silence is golden in many instances.

We must also discipline the tongue not only to absolute truth but also to the relevant truth. Be disciplined to concise, straightforward speech. Tell the truth at all times! Jesus demands total honesty from His followers:

> But above all things, my brethren, swear not, neither by heaven, neither by the earth, neither by any other oath: but let your yea be yea; and your nay, nay; lest ye fall into condemnation.
>
> James 5:12

The question of whether it is ever right to lie can be settled with this fact: God cannot lie, and He cannot delegate to you the privilege of lying for Him. When you take lies and dishonesties into your bosom, you take a fire into your soul here and hereafter.

Satan's Lie The first lie uttered in history came from the lips of Satan, the father of lies. He said to Mother Eve, "You shall not surely die" (*see* Genesis 3:4) and he has repeated this well-worn but discredited lie to every son of Adam. The truth is that something *does* die the moment you indulge in dishonesty.

89

Self-respect dies because lying is a return to a perverted nature. It is a destroyer. Death sets in and begins to gnaw at the heart the moment dishonesty steps in. We cannot get away with dishonesty.

Have you ever contemplated what would happen to society if everyone were a liar? Think about it for a moment. What if it were impossible to trust anyone? If everyone were a liar, society would destroy itself. Men of truth and fidelity hold our present society together. This also makes it possible for men of infidelity to prey upon society. Consider the following cases and see for yourself how dishonesty cancels out any good these people may have attempted to perform.

Cancelled Out   A Christian worker, a beautiful outgoing woman, would work her fingers to the bone for people at any hour of the day or night and yet she was a very lonely woman. People had discovered that she constantly told lies. That basic fault cancelled out all the good she thought she was doing.

A man of considerable talents and abilities opened a business that should have been an outstanding success. It failed. The owner lied about appointments, repairs, new equipment and so on. His dishonesty made his talents and abilities of no effect. When the word got out that he could not be trusted, the business collapsed.

I read a story of a missionary who sat and watched a man driving a cow and calf from door to door and milking the cow in the presence of the housewife. Why did he have to trudge in the hot sun day after day in this clumsy way of delivering milk? It was for a very simple reason—the man could not be trusted. He was caught watering down his milk on several different occasions and so his dishonesty doomed him to this drudgery! The moral universe had the last word.

An outstanding evangelist has left the field of evangelism because he could not tell the truth. The reports of his meetings were embellished with a few exaggerations at the beginning and gradually the exaggerations became outrageous lies. He fooled no one. The people could see for themselves—and the Lord would simply not back up his lies. Today, he is nowhere.

A Purifying Agent   Dishonesty puts sand in the internal and external machinery of life. Honesty and fidelity put oil into it. A true, faithful Christian will keep dishonesty out of his life so that he may be in constant communion with the God of truth.

A believer who has been born to new life through the Word of God must not stray from this truth once it has been accepted. Only the believer who allows himself to be habitually influenced by the indwelling of the Holy Spirit can abide in truth. When the seed of the Word abides actively in him, it acts as a purifying agent which cleanses continually, until there is freedom from dishonesty.

Think about this question for a moment: Does dishonesty in any form shock you? Examine the moral climate of your everyday life—your home, your job, your friends and your church. Is dishonesty involved in any area of your life? If the answer is *yes,* expose your sin before God and determine that in all your actions and attitudes you will speak the truth and nothing but the truth. Before long, you'll not only gain the respect of others but, more important, you'll gain the respect of the most important person in the world—you!

13
Sadness and Gloom

A group of psychologists recently conducted an investigation to determine the reasons why people consume so much alcohol. The question was asked, "Why do you drink?" The answer, "To get drunk." Just as straightforward and simple as that, "To get drunk."

But why do people deliberately want to get themselves into a state of oblivion? To people who drink to get drunk, alcohol is a cop-out. They psych themselves into thinking that alcohol will help them to forget the emptiness of their lives, to forget guilt, or to escape inner or outer dilemmas.

Is the true Christian any different? If he has the real article, he is. The Christian doesn't want to forget his former emptiness —he rejoices in his present inner fullness of life. He doesn't want to forget guilt—he remembers with joy that the Lord God has really forgiven him. He doesn't want to escape inner or outer dilemmas—he has already escaped into the arms of God where he has learned how to resolve inner dilemmas and to use and make something out of the outer ones.

In short, he has learned how to live. The pressures of life only squeeze the basic joys out of him. He has a laughter that is born of the consciousness that life approves of him, that it backs him, sustains him, and furthers him no matter what happens. He is incorrigibly happy and he doesn't get stomach ulcers. The fully surrendered Christian doesn't *try* to have a good time—he just has one.

The Mark of a Christian   Joy is the strength of the people of God—of the true Christian. If there is no real joy, there is no real Christianity. Christianity is life set to music.

Many people who consider themselves to be Christians don't seem to know anything about this—they need a very real and deep healing in their hearts. They need it and they can have it —in fact, they must have it. David said:

> But let all those that put their trust in thee rejoice: let them ever shout for joy, because thou defendest them: let them also that love thy name be joyful in thee.

Psalms 5:11

Without any doubt, joy is one of the central characteristics of the Christian. Yet, a lot of Christians know little or nothing of Christian joy. They are under the lash of duty and there is no delight in their service to the Lord. This is tragic, for there is no greater joy than knowing that we have faced up to our responsibilities and circumstances (no matter how difficult or distasteful) and have performed and fulfilled our tasks to the best of our ability.

Self-Pity   Sadness and gloom are the constant companions of those who love to float in the lake of self-pity. I counseled with a young couple confronted with the problem of a seriously retarded child—a little girl. The young mother met the whole tragedy in a spirit of faith, confidence, and love. The baby was hers and she would love and care for her no matter what the condition.

Her husband reacted differently. He was hurt deeply in the soul and spirit and didn't care who knew it. He became embittered, grew resentful against God, and wallowed in self-pity. This child would put severe limitations on his life plans. He was young and he wanted the joys of youth and the companionship of his wife.

He did not want to be shackled with the care of a retarded child and was determined to put the child away in an institution immediately. Self-pity broke up this marriage. The mother could not let go of her child. The husband would not let go of his self-pity. Two people who were once in love were left alone in the world—a world of sadness and gloom.

It is obvious that to hold self-pity is to throw a monkey wrench into the machinery of life. Structurally, you are made for positive good will. When you try the other way, then the machinery of life breaks down or works so badly that it leaves you exhausted and ineffective.

Forgiving Yourself   A businessman gave himself a little too much rope with one of his secretaries and became involved in adultery. The affair went on for a number of months until his wife got wind of it. Up until this illicit involvement, he was a respected man who had been honest in all his dealings. With the exposé, he became a changed man.

The man's wife forgave him and his children seemed to get over the initial shock of what "Dad had done." But he said, "I can see the hurt in their eyes. Things are not as they used to be."

The man became discouraged and disgusted with himself and sadness and gloom settled in on him like fog on a fall morning. He was down on himself and figured this is the way it would be for the rest of his life. The root of most of our sadness and gloom is discouragement with ourselves.

The morning he walked into my office, he was as low as a man could get. We talked. Finally, I asked him these questions: "How many years do you think it will take before you can lift up your head and forgive yourself? Have you set a definite number of years? Even murderers are eligible for parole after a certain length of time. You can keep beating yourself or you can turn to Jesus and receive genuine and complete forgiveness from Him and this, in turn, will help you to forgive yourself. The Lord Jesus Christ will wash the guilt from your conscience and you'll begin to see things in a different light."

The gentleman took my advice and we knelt before the Lord in prayer. He sobbed out his confession of sins and the Lord Jesus forgave and washed him. With the forgiveness of Christ came self-forgiveness and the sadness and gloom slipped away. The Lord Jesus gave this man back his self-respect and with it, the love of his family.

A Study of Faces   I find that the most interesting study in life is the study of faces—you ought to try it! Perhaps today, as you go about your duties, you will take the time to look into some of the faces around you. Be alert enough to be aware of what the stress of the times is doing to people.

Religious people are of particular interest. Most religious people look as if they are in great pain or as if they had eaten something quite disagreeable. Gloom and sadness is evident— grim evidence of something wrong on the inside.

I read a story of some church people who went to the railroad station to meet their new pastor whom they had never seen. They walked up to a man they thought might be him and asked, "Are you the new pastor?" The man shook his head sadly and said, "No, dyspepsia is the thing that makes me look this way."

Dyspepsia and religion which must be "endured" often put the same expression on the face. When I ask some people if they are happy and they tell me they are, then I suggest that they notify their faces.

The Covenant Community   When I study the faces of the people in the covenant community as recorded in the Book of Acts, I see people whose faces notified others that they had

94

found a deep spring of joy within. The bystanders couldn't account for this joy except on the basis that they were drunk. Peter replied, "These men are not drunken, as you suppose." They were drunk with God and the love of God; this inevitably produced inner effervescent joy. (*See* Acts 2:13–17.)

Inner unhappiness and conflict are the chief causes of confusion in the world. We project our inner unhappiness upon our surroundings and disrupt them. If you can't get along with God, you can't get along with anyone else. The early Christians that we read about in the New Testament were getting along with God, with themselves, and therefore with others. Life was set to music for them.

Bitterness   A young lady of my acquaintance felt she would never marry. No man found her attractive and wanted her. Her late teens were lived during the Korean War and just about all the young men she had known had either relocated after the war or had been killed. Life was a bore, a drag, and sadness and gloom had hit her in the face like a wet blanket. She had isolated herself and carried this deep sadness around on her face.

I spoke with this woman on a number of occasions and remarked how the look on her face would repel any eligible young men. They would run the moment they spotted her. Most people have enough problems of their own and certainly do not look for a date that would give them added problems.

One day I had my answer. It popped into my head and I feel it came directly from the Lord. This woman was blaming the Lord for her predicament. The Lord was supposed to have provided a husband for her—after all, she was a Christian and had committed her life into the hands of Jesus and He had a responsibility He did not fulfill. When I approached her with my thoughts, she admitted I was right.

I said to her, "If you feel the Lord has not done right by you, why not discuss it with Him? Why attempt to hide your feelings? Get the bitterness out and perhaps He will do something for you."

It was difficult, but she emptied out her bitterness as best she could. The bitterness was so deeply rooted that it took a number of prayer sessions together to get it out. Finally, she let go of the root and the self-pity connected with being alone. From that moment, she changed. The lines of her face turned up and she became an attractive woman again. Today, she is married and has a lovely family.

Steps to Healing   Perhaps you are saying, "Pastor Beall, you are talking to me. My life is filled with sadness and gloom. My face reflects what a mess I am on the inside. What can I do? How can I be healed? How do I get rid of my anger and self-pity and the bitterness that is in me? How do I forgive myself?"

First, you must make sure your life is in Christ—that "your life is hid with Christ in God" (*see* Colossians 3:3). This is done by getting down before the Lord and repenting of your sins and your ways. Then you must be buried with Christ in baptism. Bury the old nature, all that you have been, and rise to begin your walk in newness of life. Open your life to the tremendous infilling of the Holy Spirit.

Second, make up your mind that joy, not gloom, is your birthright as a child of God and that this is the natural way to live. You are made for joy and if there is gloom, there is something wrong.

Clear away the blocks. Name your angers and the people and things you are angry with. If you must, make a list of each one on paper and each time you go to God in prayer, confess these things to Him. You will be the one who benefits, for you will be the one who will be set free. If you are gloomy, look within, admit it, and let the Lord wash it out. If you have an unhappy home, explore the possibility of the cause being in the person your mate married. Stop blaming circumstances! (*See* chapter on Resentment.)

The Joy of the Lord   I counseled a young mother whose husband had left her and the children. He said he had no intention of returning. The woman was steaming with anger. Before we finished our session together, she was able to see herself and she laid down all her anger, bitterness and self-pity. In our next session, about two weeks later, she was a new person. She had disposed of all the poison. She was changed and the home environment was changed. It won't be long until her entire situation is changed. She now has the joy of the Lord and it works!

The next thing, make up your mind that your joy must center in God. Joy must not center in circumstances. If you center your joy in how matters go in life, you will be doomed to disappointment. Only in one place in this universe can you put your whole weight down—on God. You are joined to someone who will not change with the circumstance or times.

The Lord has been very good to me in that He has given me a good wife. Anne and I have been married for a quarter of a century now and she is one of the most even-tempered, well-balanced individuals you ever met. No matter what happens around us—in the family, in the church, in life in general—we have each other.

In this same way, we have the Lord. When our joy is centered in Him, we have it always. You will find yourself singing when you know you should be crying.

Paul at Philippi   This kind of amazing joy was seen vividly in the life of the Apostle Paul when he was in Philippi. The Philippian church was born out of pain turned to joy. Paul and Silas sat at midnight in an inner prison with backs bleeding, hands and feet in stocks, praying and singing hymns (*see* Acts 16:24, 25).

We can understand the praying, for almost everyone prays when he gets into a jam; but singing hymns! People don't do that. It was evident their joy was not in their circumstances—their joy was in the Lord. This is about as pure a spring of joy as has ever risen from the depths of human living on this planet. It was a happiness that wasn't dependent on happenings. It wasn't joy that went up like a rocket and came down like a stick. It stayed up.

The power to transform everything into joy is found today in lives surrendered in a knowledgeable way to Christ. This kind of joy can be yours. Paul said:

> Not that I speak in respect of want: for I have learned, in whatsoever state I am, therewith to be content. I know both how to be abased, and I know how to

abound: every where and in all things I am instructed both to be full and to be hungry, both to abound and to suffer need. I can do all things through Christ which strengtheneth me.

Philippians 4:11–13

Our sadness and gloom is a disappointment to the Lord because we do not believe Him nor do we look to Him for our joy. Do you remember the times when the Word of God was exceedingly sweet to your taste? Under clouds of sadness and gloom, it has become tasteless and commonplace. Without God's Word, you feel weak and wretched. With it, you grow sturdy and strong.

When in the throes of sadness and gloom, turn from complaining to a thankful attitude and begin praising God for your circumstances. This is the best remedy for you according to Proverbs 17:22: "A merry heart doeth good like a medicine: but a broken spirit drieth the bones."

14
The Material Life

Together with longevity and the respect of our fellowman, the material life forms part of the peace and fullness of life. Yet, many people find it difficult to relate the spiritual life to the material life—but it must be done if we wish to be well-balanced Christians who are going to master the problems of living. Unless this adjustment is made properly, our spiritual life will be nothing but one long series of frustrations. There are three possible ways for us to relate ourselves to the material realm:

1. We can give our lives to the pursuit of money and riches until this becomes our only aim in life.

2. We can turn our backs on the material, run from it, endeavor to live life entirely apart from it and concentrate entirely on the spiritual. (This is what many people have tried to do by shutting themselves away from society in various religious institutions.)

3. We can accept the material as God-given, dedicate it to God, and use it in such a manner as to benefit ourselves physically, mentally and spiritually, for the purposes of the Kingdom of God.

The only workable way to attain a sane balance in the realm of the material is the third way. The other two ways are unworkable and only end in disaster.

Pursuing the Material   Let us consider the first way. What happens when a life is totally dedicated to the pursuit of money and riches? Can this be done without serious repercussions? Can it bring happiness? Jesus gave a simple and pointed answer to these questions:

> Notice that, and be on your guard against covetousness in any shape or form. For a man's real life in no way depends upon the number of his possessions.

Luke 12:15 PHILLIPS

Throughout past generations, man's chief endeavor seems to have been to disprove what Jesus Christ said. Every generation that has pursued riches at the expense of everything else has suffered frustration and unhappiness. It works out that way with as much precision as two and two make four. The end result is always the same. If the basis of one's life is the material, then the basis of one's life invariably is unhappiness. Man is inherently too big to be content with a material existence. God made him that way.

The Second Attitude   On the other hand, the second attitude toward the material is as unworkable as the first. We cannot escape from the fact of the material. To ignore it completely, as though it were not present or necessary, belies the fact it is very much a part of our existence. The attempt to be either immersed in the material or to be immune to it ends in frustration.

The Balanced Way   Since true riches do not consist of what we possess, there is only one workable way of dealing with the material world. It is the Christian way of accepting what God has given in His divine generosity, and giving it to the poor. This is the rich man's responsibility. If he keeps it for himself and learns to rely upon it, He is not serving God, but mammon.

Since Jesus knew that a person who is a slave to two masters is in an impossible situation, He told us that we must make an exclusive choice between God and the riches of this world. Both are jealous masters whose interests can only clash. Concerning this matter, Jesus said:

> No one can fully serve two masters. He is bound to hate one and love the other, or be loyal to one and despise the other. You cannot serve both God and the power of money.
>
> Matthew 6:24 PHILLIPS

Does this mean we are to renounce everything we have and own? No, definitely *no!* This is one of the errors that has crept into the present-day Jesus Movement. The people involved either sell or give away everything they have and go off to live in a commune where they resort to begging for bread, or expect God to send down manna from heaven. This is wrong! Prosperity is the result of effort, a sign of accomplishment.

If it is God who enriches us, does it not follow that the things He has given us are a consequence of His blessing? When we become the children of God, He desires to fulfill us completely that we may lack nothing. The words of the Twenty-third Psalm illustrate clearly the fullness of life which God bestows upon His elect:

Because the Lord is my Shepherd, I have everything
I need! He lets me rest in the meadow grass and leads
me beside the quiet streams. He restores my failing
health. He helps me do what honors him the most.
Even when walking through the dark valley of death
I will not be afraid, for you are close beside me, guard-
ing, guiding all the way. You provide delicious food for
me in the presence of my enemies. You have wel-
comed me as your guest; blessings overflow! Your
goodness and unfailing kindness shall be with me all of
my life, and afterwards I will live with you forever in
your home.

Psalms 23 LB

The fullness of God is perfection in abundance—it is totality.
In Jesus, in whom lives the complete fullness of God, are hidden
all the treasures in superabundance. These treasures cannot be
compared with hoarded and avariciously preserved riches, but
are like living waters which swell, overflow, and break loose.

In Him is the fullness of life which takes away the sting of the
emptiness of death. In Him is power which pours salvation to
the lost; sanctification to His Body, the Church; and wisdom, a
treasure superior to all else, which He communicates to whom-
ever He wishes.

Controlling the Material   To the Christian, life is Christ
and everything else is mastered and subordinated to serve
Christ. To many people, life is food. To the sensualist, life is
emotion. To the materialist, life is money. These are the controlling factors in their lives. They are controlled by things—by
food, by emotion, and by money.

Those of us who name the Name of Christ are to do the
controlling of things. We must not be controlled by them! If we
allow ourselves to be controlled by a thing, a thirst develops for
it and, in time, it will dominate us completely.

There is a proverb (not a biblical one) which says, "Whosoever craves wealth is like a man who drinks sea water; the more

he drinks, the more he increases his thirst, and he ceases not to drink until he perishes." This is very true. Life bears it out.

Acquiring Things   If a man spends his whole life saving enough money to buy a car which he can drive to work, one might feel that this man's life is wasted. Yet, many do exactly this. They may acquire more *things* than a car but their entire life is directed toward the acquisition of more and more objects.

A friend of mine has become *thing-crazy*. He has little regard for the quality of the products he buys or their usefulness to him. What is important to him is quantity. If someone he knows has more than he does, he feels slighted and will go into debt to outdo the other person.

Has this brought the man happiness? Certainly not! He has developed an ulcer and very serious family problems. Yet, for some odd reason, he will not stop long enough to examine his relationship to the objects he acquires. He doesn't seem to realize that his lust for possessions is the seed of his own unhappiness. Advertising, television, and movies tell him that if he is unhappy, he should go out and buy something. So the man goes on and on—a boat, two new cars, cottages, motorcycles, snowmobiles—the list goes on forever.

Foolishly, he continues to believe and hope almost religiously that one more possession might bring him the happiness and peace that seem to fade further away with every passing day. This man's faith was placed in material things; objects that rust, corrode, and break or wear out in just a short time.

What, then, should the object of his faith and hope be? He needs something that won't go out of style, or break down, or wear out, or rust, or lose its value. He needs something eternal.

Illusions of Wealth   Jesus zeroed in on my friend's problem when He mentioned the two things which choked the growing wheat and caused it to be unfruitful:

> The seed sown among the thorns represents the man who hears the message, and then the worries of this life

and the illusions of wealth choke it to death and so it produces no "crop" in his life.

Matthew 13:22 PHILLIPS

Here, worries and the illusions of wealth are classed as the two outstanding enemies of growth of the human personality and growth in the Kingdom of God. The seed, which is the doctrine of the Kingdom, cannot come to maturity if side by side with it grows preoccupation with the affairs of the world and particularly with the seductive glamour of riches.

Please note: Christ did not call riches *Enemy Number One* but He called them *illusions of wealth.* When wealth becomes an end in itself, a man has been deceived. The delight is centered upon the thing itself rather than upon what it could do. This is the way of undedicated wealth. We must master wealth and not allow wealth to master us!

How do we go about mastering this matter of money? What are we to do? The first thing we must do is to stop and think: Who is God? If God is the Creator of the universe and our Creator, then remember: "The earth is the Lord's and the fulness thereof . . ." (Psalms 24:1). We do not own the earth, God does. The regulation of our lives should be upon His shoulders and not upon ours. We cannot run the world. God runs things and He certainly can take care of us.

Tithing   To this point, we have learned two important things: (1) God does not want us to live in poverty and (2) He does not want us to place too much emphasis on material things. God is a God of balance. He does not ask the impossible of us. All He asks us to do is acknowledge that what we have comes from Him, and giving the first 10 percent of our income to the Lord symbolizes that the remaining nine-tenths belongs to Him also. This is what tithing is all about.

In Hebrew history, the people waved the first fruits of the harvest before the Lord as acknowledgement that the coming harvest belonged to Him and that they would use it as such. The people did not always do as intended but this was the initial purpose of their offering. Often, they would pursue the Jewish custom of offering a chicken to God, placing their sins on the chicken and throwing it under the table. From there the chicken would disappear and the next time it was seen it was on the table ready to be eaten! In doing so, they ended up defeated, for this was man's way of doing things, not God's way. If we give to God in His way, we will have balance and happiness.

A Giving Spirit   No one in the world can be happy unless he learns the secret of giving. There must be a "give" in our spirits—toward God and toward man. The Kingdom principle is to give:

> Give, and it shall be given unto you; good measure, pressed down, and shaken together, and running over, shall men give into your bosom. For with the same measure that ye mete withal it shall be measured to you again.

> Luke 6:38

This is so very true, it is frightening. If we have a "give" in our spirits, people want us around, not because of what we give them but because we are pleasant, outgoing personalities. One who is tightfisted with money is tightfisted in every aspect of life.

Because we have received so very, very much from God, giving to others should take on such fullness and intensity in our lives that those who are the recipients thank God for His generosity. Whether we give material goods or spiritual gifts, we are to look upon them as riches which have been entrusted to us for the service of others and of which we are merely the stewards.

When Jesus made the disciples the stewards of the loaves and fishes, suppose what would have happened had they said to themselves, "Let's not serve this food; let's save it for ourselves. We'll corner this abundant food supply and make the multitude, driven by hunger, pay us for it. We have a real case of supply and demand here. We would be foolish not to take advantage of it."

What do you think would have happened? The disciples' connection with heaven would have been broken—that's what would have happened! If they had stopped giving out, they would have stopped receiving. Christ kept giving them food as long as they kept giving it out.

Others Who Gave   On the day we commemorate as Palm Sunday, the Lord Jesus needed a colt upon which to ride. What if the man who owned the colt had refused to give it to the disciples? Supposing he had said, "What do you mean, the Lord hath need of him? I have need of him; he is mine. Don't touch that animal or I will have you arrested."

What would have been the result of such a lack of *give* in the man? I believe for the rest of his days he would have had an inner conflict over that day and that colt, trying to justify the unjustifiable. But the man did have a *give* in him and when his colt was returned to him, it became the most famous colt in history. Can you imagine all the rich stories the man told about that animal?

Suppose the little boy had refused to let Christ have his five loaves and fishes, saying he was hungry and needed them for himself. I am sure he would have hated himself for the rest of his days. Jesus was going to feed that multitude, one way or another. It was just a matter of who would allow the Master to use what they had to give. That little boy became the center of gratitude of five thousand people and the center of inner peace because he gave what he had.

The Lord God affords us many such opportunities. How many times could He have used our money to feed multitudes but we refused to disturb our nest egg and so He turned to someone else? Many people are lean in their souls simply because they are lean toward others. They receive exactly what they measure out.

Greed and Lust   As Christians, we must learn to master what God has given us and use it sensibly, that it may be profitable to us physically, mentally and spiritually. In Proverbs, Agur asks God for help in this area:

. . . give me neither poverty nor riches! Give me just enough to satisfy my needs! For if I grow rich, I may become content without God. And if I am too poor, I may steal, and thus insult God's holy name.

Proverbs 30:8,9

God will provide for His own but if there is greed or lust, He will see it. You may think that you are getting what you want and that may be true, but God knows what you need. To show you your own greed, He may give you the Midas touch. Examine yourself. Are you being blessed by God for true service and humility? Or is your greed and lust masked by material satisfaction? Are you at peace in your mind and in your home?

God may be setting you up so that your own greed will knock you down. A child gets sick on too much candy but often doesn't know when to stop. Be wise! Keep money and material objects in their rightful place—as aids to comfort, not as brightly painted detours on the road to peace and happiness.

Put your money to work for the glory of the Kingdom of God. In this way, you will be laying up treasures for eternity, treasures that will never pass away.

15
Guilt

Guilt feelings are unpleasant feelings of sinfulness that manifest themselves when our behavior and desires do not conform to our moral standards. When we fail to live up to our ethical and moral values, self-condemnation plays havoc with our feelings of security and adequacy. Severe self-devaluation is not mutually compatible with good mental and physical health.

Guilt is a strange and tormenting malady that is found in all cultures and affects all of us to some degree. We all do things which we later regret and for which we condemn ourselves. Much effort is put forth to analyze the thoughts, minds, and souls of men that they might find relief from the mental anguish that guilt brings. If it is not handled properly, it can lead a man or woman to destruction.

Feelings of guilt can work for our good in one respect, yet be totally destructive in another. Many people have become reactionaries when it comes to spiritual things. In times past, they have heard old-time evangelism put a great deal of emphasis upon guilt, but the point that was stressed was what happened to the guilty when they died.

The great question was: As a guilty soul, how will you stand before the throne of God? This particular emphasis didn't appeal to very many people so they just cast it aside and continued in their old way of life. They didn't realize that unless guilt is removed, man must somehow learn to live with it and tolerate it. Guilt will either lead you to God or it will be the means of your destruction.

Releasing the Guilt   Facing guilt is necessary if we are to face up to life. Our God is a God of great grace. For this we are very thankful! We know God will pardon any man who will come to Him, confess his sins out of an honest heart and really mean business with God. The problem with most religious seekers today is that they do not mean business with God.

A question which Christ frequently asked seekers in His day also applies to our particular hour: Will you be made whole? Is it your honest desire to be released? Do you want to walk with God or are you just seeking His favor that you might walk more conveniently in your own way?

Many people who desire spiritual release know that a responsibility comes with the release, yet they still hope to have the opportunity to pursue their own desires. When God intervenes in a life by bringing healing and release, the individual becomes responsible to and for the Kingdom of God. Whenever the goodness of the Kingdom comes to a man, his attitude toward the Kingdom must change. From that moment on, he is responsible to put the Kingdom of God first in his life.

Sowing Wild Oats   We live in a day when the word *sin* has almost lost its meaning. To some the word is only a religious platitude; to others it suggests intrigue, fascination, and exploration. Modern thought tells us to obey our instincts or we will be plagued with inhibitions. Just go ahead and express yourself. Sow your wild oats! Don't allow anyone to put a damper on your spirits or a halter on your neck. Throw restraint and caution to the wind! Live life to its fullest! *Nothing could be more deceiving than this theory! Nothing could be more destructive!*

A young psychiatrist made a practice of advising women who were distraught and nervous to find a male friend and have a good time. His patients foolishly took his advice and committed adultery. Soon they found themselves so steeped in guilt and anguish that their homes were destroyed. Not only was this the plight of the patients but the prominent doctor himself became the victim of his theory. By loose, uninhibited indulgence in sin, the very people he was trying to heal were destroyed and he was also destroyed.

The Guilt of David   In the Psalms, we have the written account of David, who was king over the land of Israel yet allowed himself too much liberty when it came to controlling his emotions. He let his emotions run rampant and committed adultery. In the sight of God, David sinned.

As a result of his sin, guilt closed in on him. It drove him to distraction. David lost contact with God! The overshadowing presence of God was gone. David was on the barren end of nowhere. He cried out, "My God, have mercy upon me. According to thy loving kindness, according to thy tender mercies, blot out my transgressions. Wash me thoroughly from my iniquities, and cleanse me from my sin" (*see* Psalms 51:1,2).

By this honest, sincere confession of his sins, David found release from guilt—and favor with God. David found he could not hide sin and neither could he live with it. The only answer was pardon, release, and cleansing from God. In spite of all the wrongs David had committed—adultery, murder—God loved him so much that when He spoke of him, He would say:

> . . . to keep my statutes and my judgments as did David.
> . . . I will make him prince all the days of his life for
> David my servant's sake, whom I chose, because he
> kept my commandments and my statutes. . . . And it
> shall be, if thou wilt hearken unto all that I command
> thee, and wilt walk in my ways, and do that is right in
> my sight, to keep my statutes and my commandments,
> as David my servant did; that I will be with thee, and
> build thee a sure house, as I built for David. . . .
>
> 1 Kings 11:33,34,38

David seemed to be a man after God's own heart because he did not attempt to justify himself or make excuses for his sins. He acknowledged his wrongdoings and confessed them for the sins they were.

A Defiled Conscience   This is exactly what guilt is: a defilement of the conscience. And to be plagued by a guilty conscience is utter misery. The conscience becomes an offense to God because of the transgression. Through our conscience, we knew what was right but we preferred to do wrong. We went ahead anyway and walked into sin with our eyes wide open. We knew we were wrong the moment we took the first step but that first step led to the second step and soon we committed sin.

The Bible says: "Sin is a willful transgression of the law" (*see* 1 John 3:4). Guilt comes as a result of sin. Guilt will torment you; it will harass you; it will drag you down and make you old before your years. You can never learn to live with it and it cannot be shaken off. You cannot rid yourself of guilt by telling yourself that sin is just a figment of the mind. Christ is the only answer for a defiled conscience.

Guilt is not a disease of the uneducated; it is just as prevalent among the intellectual as among the ignorant. It strikes the rich as well as the poor, the young and the old, the civilized and the uncivilized. Its cause is a troubled conscience. It is the result of sin against God when we had the knowledge to do right!

Multitudes today could have release from guilt if they would do one thing: acknowledge their sins before God. If you try to cover them up and call them something else, your guilt will be retained. In so doing, you deny yourself deliverance from guilt. Your release will only come if you honestly go before God and pour out your heart, saying, "Lord, I have sinned against Thee. I have done evil in Your sight. I know You desire truth in the inner parts for in the inner parts of a man You make wisdom known."

Hampered by Guilt   I have never been able to help a person hampered by guilt by heaping criticism upon him. The Lord God knew this before I ever did. Many religious people have the idea that God holds out on us until we meet certain requirements to earn His forgiveness of sins and removal of guilt. To these people, the Bible speaks only of an angry God who loves to criticize and punish rather than a God of infinite grace who provides forgiveness and cleansing.

A man of my acquaintance came to see me at a time of real crisis in his life. His children were leaving home as soon as they were grown up enough to do so. While at home, there was no love lost between child and parent. The children complained, "He is always critical; he doesn't trust us and accuses us constantly of being bent on sex and unclean things."

The man defended his actions by saying, "This is what God expects a father to be. A man has to keep his kids in line or he answers to God."

I asked him, "What are you afraid they will do? Are you afraid they will do what you've done?"

He was indignant. After a while, his fury subsided and he began to soften. As the words began to roll, he admitted he had been a wild kid and became involved in many things which, in time, had become a source of shame and disgust to him. Whenever he associated himself, in age, with his children, he suffered the pangs of guilt. Because of his guilt, he became critical of his children.

I pointed out to him that when love is low, criticism is high and if he would allow the love of Christ to break in upon him, he would have a new concept of God and of himself as a father.

As this man found the love of God, he became a changed person. His guilt melted away through love and consequently the criticism that ran rampant in that family is now at an all-time low.

A Strange Land of Captivity   When a man is consumed by guilt, he has no song, no joy, no happiness. All joy of living is gone. I maintain that when a Christian loses his song, there is a reason. We always lose our song when we are in a strange land of captivity. David said, "Make me to hear joy and gladness; that the bones which thou has broken may rejoice" (Psalms 51:8).

Guilt drove David to a place where he sought God in a new way. Yes, he wanted his sins forgiven and the guilt removed, but now he was crying, "Create in me a clean heart, O God; and renew a right spirit within me" (Psalms 51:10). The only hope for David was to give himself wholly and completely to God.

Our only hope is to give ourselves wholly and completely to Christ. Why is this? Because He is the only one who can create in us a new heart and a right spirit. A doctor cannot do this; no human can do this. David was wise. He did not ask the Lord to teach him how to live with his evil, deceptive heart. Oh, no! He knew he needed a change of heart, mind, and spirit and this is what he asked of God!

Our Mediator   Christ is the only answer to guilt. He is the only remedy for sin. Jesus Christ died on the Cross of Calvary and shed His blood that He might open the way for all mankind into the very presence of God. The sins we have committed are against God and we must confess them to Him to receive forgiveness and pardon. The Scriptures tell us we can only come into the presence of the Father through His Son, the Lord Jesus, who, as the risen Christ, is mediating in our behalf. We can go directly to Christ by faith and He will plead our case before the Father:

For there is one God, and one mediator between God and men, the man Christ Jesus; Who gave himself a ransom for all, to be testified in due time.

1 Timothy 2:5, 6

Confessing our sins to God will bring the cleansing power of the blood of Christ upon our hearts and minds. By this cleansing, an amazing thing happens: Our transgressions are removed and the guilt is purged from our conscience. What relief! The guilt and condemnation of sin is gone!

A New Heart   But, wait a minute. Let's go a step further. Thank God the sin and condemnation is removed, but what about the new heart and right spirit? Right here is where the vast majority of people are failing. Their sins are forgiven, the guilt is gone, but they pick up their old way of life again.

The forgiveness of sins is not the end of God's salvation! He has a new way of life for us. The very purpose of having your sins forgiven is to make you fit for this new walk in the Spirit. After we are cleansed from our sins, we become new creatures in Christ Jesus and a new creature must have a new heart and a new spirit!

In fact, this is the promise of the New Covenant. The new heart is what the Bible calls a circumcised heart. The human heart is circumcised spiritually by Christ when the believer is baptized into Christ in water baptism. This baptism is more than a ritual or a form; it is a necessary step of obedience by which salvation continues to work that we might be brought to maturity in Jesus Christ. Here is the Scripture:

In whom also ye are circumcised with the circumcision made without hands, in putting off the body of the sins of the flesh by the circumcision of Christ: [when you were] Buried with him in baptism, wherein also ye are risen with him through the faith of the operation of God, who hath raised him from the dead.

Colossians 2:11,12

112

Obedience to Christ is the way of life and peace. After baptism is administered, every believer must be filled or baptized with the Holy Spirit to become a useful instrument of God. Don't seek to be rid of guilt just to be free to go on your own merry way. Seek to be used and energized by God so that others, too, can be lifted up into new realms of glory.

False Guilt   To those who are the victims of false guilt, it is necessary to point out that this type of guilt is as destructive as real guilt because it keeps the individual in bondage and blocks spiritual growth. False guilt torments many sincere people, accusing them constantly. This guilt must be shed if the believer desires to move on with God.

Some people feel guilty simply because they are tempted—everyone is tempted! We are not immune to temptation but we are promised a way of escape through the Lord Jesus Christ. The Bible tells us:

> There hath no temptation taken you but such as is common to man: but God is faithful, who will not suffer you to be tempted above that ye are able; but will with the temptation also make a way to escape, that ye may be able to bear it.

> 1 Corinthians 10:13

Jesus was also tempted. It is said of Him that He was tempted in all points such as you and I are, yet without sin (*see* Hebrews 4:15).

Temptation is not sin, so shed that guilt! Shake it off! Refuse to labor under it! Perhaps you have been tempted with unclean thoughts. If you have, turn your thoughts to pure things and in doing so, you will not commit sin.

Some poor souls live in torment thinking they have committed the "unpardonable sin." Usually, this guilt is false. The unpardonable sin of which Jesus Christ spoke was to call the works of the Holy Spirit the works of Beelzebub! (*See* Matthew 12:22–32.) Some even said that the Holy Spirit was an unclean spirit.

113

Examine yourself in the light of the Word of God. If your feeling of guilt is without reason, throw it off. God intended we should be free and has made abundant provision for our freedom. How wonderful to know we can be free from the torment of guilt.

If you have sinned, if your guilt is based on willfully entertaining a sinful thought, word, or deed, come to Jesus now and confess it. You will find reconciliation, forgiveness, and assurance in Christ Jesus our Lord.

16
Stress

An article written by a doctor suggests the theory that the basis of all diseases is stress. The doctor became interested not in specific diseases but in the possible cause of all diseases—something that lay back of everything. He fastened on stress.

Whenever an obstacle blocks our drive toward some socially approved goal, we experience biological or psychological stress or a combination of the two. Stress situations impose upon us mental or physical strain because they deny the satisfaction of certain needs. The sources of stress are many: pain, fatigue, grief, anxiety, suffering, disease, insecurity, physical handicaps, insufficient intelligence, and a variety of other adversities.

When a person is under biological stress, the glands throw their secretions into the system to maintain the balance of the organism. If the stress persists over a long period of time, the body chemistry and often psychological functioning is impaired. When that happens, disease may break out anywhere in the body.

Here is an illustration: When pneumonia viruses invade the human body, the brain sounds an alarm "calling to arms" the body's defense forces. The leucocytes (white blood corpuscles) then move in to destroy the disease-causing viruses. If the on-slaught of the pneumonia viruses occurs during a severe stress situation, this process is disrupted. The glands secrete excessive amounts of unnecessary hormones into the bloodstream, upset-ting the chemical equilibrium. This defeats the work of the leucocytes as they attempt to engulf the viruses. The end result: pneumonia. The cause back of it all is stress.

Unbearable Stress   To cite a case in point, a young lady came to see me and complained of suffering severe migraine headaches which were affecting her vision. Her doctor told her she needed spiritual counseling. There were many problems in her life that needed to be resolved.

Her husband was an unstable man who drifted from one job position to another and would do little or nothing around the house. Two grade-school children were her complete responsi-bility. Some days the stress of looking into a dark and dismal future was too much for her. The mind would not take the stress and her headaches would become unbearable. Gradually, they affected her sight. She was caught. She was a brokenhearted woman who was asking God to help her.

In the Scriptures, the young lady was shown that if she would give herself to Jesus Christ, He would take watchful care of her. The Lord would supply her needs for He has never left His children in the streets to beg bread. He said:

> But even the very hairs of your head are all numbered.
> . . . Consider the ravens: for they neither sow nor reap;
> which neither have storehouse nor barn; and God
> feedeth them: how much more are ye better than the
> fowls? . . . And seek ye not what ye shall eat, or what
> ye shall drink, neither be ye of doubtful mind. . . . But
> rather seek ye the kingdom of God; and all these things
> shall be added unto you.
>
> Luke 12:7, 24, 29, 31

At first, she found this difficult to believe. It was a complete reversal of her thinking. Her husband would not take care of

115

her properly and satisfy her needs so she was completely self-preoccupied in taking care of herself. As I showed her how she had entered the world of self-preoccupation and how to walk out of it by becoming occupied with Jesus Christ and the Kingdom of God, the lines of her face began to lose their tightness.

We knelt at the office couch and she placed her life into the hands of Christ. She changed her thinking. She stopped taking care of herself. She surrendered herself to Christ and became receptive. She was instructed that whenever she was tempted to take the reins of her life—with its stress and pressures—back into her own hands she should stop, kneel before God, and once again place the government of her life on the shoulders of Jesus Christ.

In a matter of weeks the headaches were gone, her sight restored to normal, and she was singing. Not only this, but she is a new wife to her husband and a new mother to her children. The house had become a relaxed home—the Kingdom of God had come and the brokenhearted had been healed.

Psychological Stress   As mentioned earlier, stress occurs on a psychological as well as a biological level. In psychological stress, we find two types of defenses: (1) reactions which involve the use of our mental faculties in making effective adjustment that will solve problems and gratify needs and (2) ego defense mechanisms which are unconscious devices we use to protect our self-esteem.

The first type of defense is used to perceive the conditions of the situation, and our reaction to it is strongly influenced by the ideas we have developed about ourselves and the world around us. The way in which we think, learn, and reason will determine the outcome of the situation.

Ego defense mechanisms are comparable with the way the body maintains its chemical balance but instead of secreting hormones, the brain protects the individual from humiliating failure by alleviating or solving the problem through indirect means. These defenses are necessary cop-outs which we gradually build up around us to protect the self from insult and to enhance it as much as we possibly can.

Although these defense mechanisms are essential for maintaining our feeling of adequacy and personal worth, for softening our failures, and for protecting us from anxiety, they do have their drawbacks. They cause us to deceive ourselves and to distort reality. If we continually rationalize our mistakes, we will not learn from them.

Ego Defense Mechanisms   To help us understand what ego defense mechanisms are and how they help us to cope with stress situations, I give the following examples:

1. *Fantasy*—Through daydreaming, the individual escapes from reality into a fantasy world where he allows his imagination to fulfill his goals and gratify his needs.

2. *Denial of reality*—The unpleasant aspects of reality are ignored by refusing to acknowledge that they exist.

3. *Compensation*—An attempt is made to disguise or cover up an undesired trait by exaggerating a desired trait.

4. *Identification*—An emotional tie with an individual or institution of a successful nature causes a person to think, act, and feel as he imagines the person or institution would expect.

5. *Introjection*—The person incorporates external events into his own psyche and reacts to them as though they were internal. For instance, although there is no physical cause, the person suffers the same pains as another.

6. *Projection*—An unconscious act or process attributes to others the blame for one's difficulties or one's own unethical desires or impulses.

7. *Rationalization*—the person thinks up "good" reasons to justify what he has done, is doing, or intends to do, usually without being aware of the real motives.

8. *Repression*—Dangerous desires and intolerable memories are kept out of the conscious.

9. *Displacement*—Transfer or redirection of an emotion is made from one object or person to another. It usually involves discharging negative emotions toward a less dangerous object or person. Instead of taking out hostility on the boss, it is taken out on the spouse.

10. *Emotional insulation*—The person withdraws into a

shell of passivity to reduce the tensions of need and anxiety.

11. *Isolation*—The person disassociates or cuts himself off from a hurtful situation by breaking ties or connections with the threatening conditions or persons.

12. *Regression*—Less mature responses are used in attempting to cope with stress and maintaining ego integrity.

13. *Undoing*—This includes penance, repentance, punishment, and apologizing for wrongs committed in an effort to make up for or atone for misdeeds.

14. *Sublimation*—Frustrated sexual energy is channelled partially into constructive, socially approved forms.

When we experience psychological stress, the ego defense mechanisms are threatened and the longer the stress lasts, the more severe it is. The more important the need that is being thwarted, the greater will be the stress. Stress situations force us to do something and always require some sort of adjustment to be made. An important factor to consider in determining the severity of the stress is the individual's evaluation of the stress situation.

Oppressive Authority   Another area where stress seems to bring a great deal of illness and physical problems is the area of oppressive authority—on the job, in the home, in church. Oppressive authority can bring you to smoldering resentment, hatred, and the deep desire to strike back. It can and will make you sick if you do not learn how to handle it.

How did the early Christians handle this matter? Can we learn a modern-day lesson from them? I think so! The early Christian movement was caught between the oppressive religious authority of Judaism and the oppressive military authority of the Roman Empire. The clash with oppressive authority is seen in these words:

> . . . and when they had called the apostles, and beaten them, they commanded that they should not speak in the name of Jesus, and let them go. And they departed from the presence of the council, rejoicing that they were counted worthy to suffer shame for his name.

And daily in the temple, and in every house, they ceased not to teach and preach Jesus Christ.

Acts 5:40–42

The clash with authority was clear-cut and decisive and their response was just as clear-cut and decisive.

They knew that if they could keep their inner life clean and clear, they would not contaminate their covenant society through their hatred, anger, and resentment. They had to keep their commission free. They decided to serve God and honor the Name of Jesus and let the Lord God take care of Judaism and the Romans.

The important lesson to learn here is that they did not sulk, become self-preoccupied, and feel sorry for themselves. They determined not to be a sick society hiding out from oppressive authority and for this reason they became a healing power rather than a sick, disintegrating nothing.

Oppressive Circumstances   There are some people who do not live under oppressive authority, but rather under oppressive circumstances which are making them sick. The silent pressures of incompatibility, alcoholism, unfaithfulness, and constant nagging are driving great numbers up the wall.

There are three remedies—one, to run away; another, to retreat completely within. Both are the attitudes of a defeatist. The third is the strongly suggested remedy, namely, to secure your base by full surrender to God and by quieting yourself. Then look for a creative outlet in God so you will not be tempted to wallow in the pond of self-pity and self-preoccupation.

Limitations in Life   Next, you must understand that everyone lives his life under certain limitations. No one has a clear field to live life completely as he likes. There are too many other human wills around us.

Jesus Christ had to live His life out under limitations and oppositions in the cramping environment of a provincial village such as Nazareth. The account says that, in spite of the limitations, ". . . Jesus increased in wisdom and stature, and in favour with God and man" (Luke 2:52). His limited environment did not thwart Him or turn Him inward. Christ used every circumstance as an emery wheel to make Him sharp. In all of the circumstances, He learned.

What have *you* learned about life and helping people through the circumstances which have come to you? Perhaps you say, "I haven't learned from them because I hate them!" All right, has hating made you well or sick?

But you say, "I feel I have been betrayed. I was given promises. I expected a good life. I did not expect hell."

The Bible says of Jesus, " . . . the Lord Jesus the same night in which he was betrayed took bread" (1 Corinthians 11:23). Christ turned a betrayal into a sacrament. The betrayal passed away. The sacrament lives on. Jesus turned the betrayal into something good. He did not allow it to sour Him and it must not sour you. If it has, it is because you have become self-preoccupied. The Lord was taken up with the salvation of the world. The betrayal could be either a stepping-stone or a stumbling block and it dare not be the latter. The same applies to you.

Wrong Thinking   Get your eyes on wrong things and, in time, they will make you sick. This is true of churches as well as individuals. In the Book of Revelation is a picture of a church that was better at hating than loving.

> . . . . I know you don't tolerate sin among your members, and you have carefully examined the claims of those who say they are apostles but aren't. You have found out how they lie. You have patiently suffered for me without quitting. Yet there is one thing wrong; you don't love me as at first!
>
> Revelation 2:2–4 LB

These Christians were good at intolerance of sin but they were poor at loving. They were negative. Consequently, they were in the process of decay. Too many churches are like this.

I know a minister with outstanding gifts of oratory and seem-

120

ing persuasion but I questioned myself on a number of occasions as to why he was not more successful. Following a meeting, I received my answer. He said, "Well, I guess I pricked a few balloons tonight!"

It suddenly dawned on me: His abilities are dedicated to breaking balloons. When this was accomplished, what was left? Nothing positive! The man was sick and he was making others spiritually ill. Many were enamored when they first heard him but soon left when they realized a steady diet of negatives would only kill their spiritual incentive.

Right Thinking   There is little doubt that right thinking is important if we want to overcome the problems of stress. The Apostle Paul said:

> Finally, brethren, whatsoever things are true, whatsoever things are honest, whatsoever things are just, whatsoever things are pure, whatsoever things are lovely, whatsoever things are of good report; if there be any virtue, and if there be any praise, think on these things. Those things, which ye have both learned, and received, and heard, and seen in me, do: and the God of peace shall be with you.
>
> Philippians 4:8, 9

Karl Menninger, head of the famous clinic at Topeka, Kansas, names four things necessary to mental and physical health: creative work, creative play, creative worship, and creative love. This is exactly what Paul is saying: each person must find something outside of himself.

If work, play, worship, and love are not creative, producing something constructive outside of the individual, the person is vulnerable to stress and the diseases of the body that result. If any of these four creative outlets leave you in a state of self-preoccupation, examine the particular area carefully and seek to find ways of satisfying your needs in positive, socially approved practices.

I have found in my years of observing sick and needy people

that one of the most needed deliverances is from self-preoccupation. Sickness will almost always bring your full attention to yourself and this is damaging and harmful, to say the least. If people can turn themselves to God and begin to love God and others instead of themselves, their chances of recovery will increase greatly.

If we want healing and release from stress, we must learn to practice positive attitudes of mind and emotions. The effects of thought and emotion reach down into every cell of the body and affect them for good or ill. In all of the problems connected with stress, we must continually keep stepping out of the circle of preoccupation. With the help of God, you can begin to end your hassle with stress. Do it now.

Lord Jesus, today I take a deliberate step out of the circle of preoccupation. I determine, by Your strength, to turn every and all circumstances into an emery board to sharpen me. I am not going to allow my life to be blocked by circumstances and things and I am going to do things for others instead of complaining about my own situation. I want to learn through life and circumstances, honestly, I do. Thoughtfully and deeply, I give my life to You. Amen.

17
Depression

The *Wall Street Journal* has called depression the "disease of the 70s." Most of us have suffered depression at one time or another, usually in the wake of some traumatic experience or terrible loss. Most depression runs its course in time and is gone.

Serious forms of depression afflict from four to eight million

Americans, according to some medical sources. Many of these depressive Americans will recover. Some of them won't—they'll just give up. A great number of those who are hospitalized will simply turn their faces to the wall and drop from the real world. Others will take their own lives.

Some of the factors which may throw us headlong into depression are familiar to each of us: death, loss, rejection, separation from those we love, illness, failure in marriage, work, or school, financial setbacks, and old age.

Symptoms of Depression   Physicians have been describing depression since the days of Hippocrates. He called it "melancholia." Although the symptoms of depression are many and varied, the most prominent symptom is passivity—nothing really seems to matter. Passivity breeds other negative responses such as: a slowdown of response, loss of interest, decrease in energy, an inability to accomplish tasks, difficulty in concentration, and the erosion of motivation and ambition. During this time, an individual may experience feelings of unworthiness, sinfulness, guilt, and utter hopelessness; a lack of appetite; constipation; digestive problems; sleeplessness; and various other bodily ailments. When the depression becomes acute, the person tends to isolate himself from everyone because the simplest daily tasks begin to sap his strength and energy.

For many depressives, the first signs of illness are in the area of their increasing inability to cope with their work and responsibilities. The will becomes seriously muddled. They desire to snap out of it, but can't pull it off. In severe cases there is complete paralysis of the will. We can't afford this. Consequently, we must deal with depression in its elementary stages while our will is active and strong.

Most people who become depressed and remain in their depression for considerable lengths of time have come to a point in life where they feel helpless in the light of their situation. This feeling of helplessness develops into a belief. They believe and are certain that nothing can be done about their problem. They turn to despair.

A Disease of Today   Depression in the seventies has reached into every stratum of society. Many clinicians have reported an increasing pervasiveness of depression among college students. This seems strange when you consider the many stimulations they have been afforded—more sex, more intellectual stimulation, more cars, more music, more of everything than any previous generation. Why should they be depressed?

They say their depression lies in the fact that they have not done anything significant and they feel helpless in doing anything of consequence. Someone said, "Rewards as well as punishments that come independently of one's own effort can be depressing."

Perhaps this is the reason many beautiful women attempt suicide. They have received attention because of their glamour and so-called sex appeal but they have not experienced anything in the realm of personal achievement. Instinctively, they have a problem with guilts and depression.

Others have problems with depression in spite of their high achievements. Students in graduate programs have been known to fall into deep depression once they have reached their goal. Where do you go from here? Having a doctoral degree has not produced anything magical. They remain the same person they were before they started. Depression often follows.

Disturbed Family Relations   What causes people to crawl into a shell and look upon themselves as social outcasts? A child looks to his all-powerful and all-knowing parents for love and acceptance. When there is active and open rejection on the part of one or both parents, the child sees himself as a worthless, wicked, unacceptable, and repulsive creature.

He suffers from feelings of isolation, inadequacy, and inferiority. He feels no one cares about him and that he is unimportant. When he has problems or needs, he learns to stand alone, not expecting anything from anyone. The rejected child becomes vulnerable to stresses which could probably be handled readily were he not so handicapped. In later life, he will have difficulty expressing and responding to affection.

The child whose personality is crippled by rejection becomes so emotionally handicapped that he is almost overcome by hostility toward the person he sees as the source of his frustration. He wants to impair, destroy, or damage the person but this kind of hostility is too dangerous for him to express. Instead, he represses it in order to gain the favor of his parents.

This means that, at all costs, he must avoid all unnecessary friction that might result in parental retaliation. Instead of being able to stand up for his own rights, the child must learn to tolerate and accept the injustices heaped upon him by the parents.

Antisocial behavior such as lying, stealing, promiscuity, and all types of delinquency are the child's weapons of open rebellion against the parents. The dangerous impulses that have been repressed may erupt into violent behavior.

Individuals who have been rejected by their parents tend to be fearful, jealous, attention-seeking, hostile, and lonely. As adults, they withdraw from social situations because they are hurt and scared. This withdrawal does not necessarily reduce their need or desire for social approval and love. They withdraw because the fear of rejection is far stronger than the desire for acceptance.

The end result of rejection is an insecure individual who evaluates the world as a dangerous place, and therefore, withdraws himself from it. The emotions and feelings which accompany the experience of rejection often lead to depression. In fact, few experiences can be as devastating as rejection, whether this rejection is of child by parent (or vice versa) or an adult by members of his or her social circle.

An Impossible Situation   One interview I had with a young man will, I think, stay with me for a lifetime. The boy was depressed most of the time and this had been going on most of his life. The depression was due to rejection by both his parents. He knew his parents loved him in their own way but they vehemently rejected the kind of person he was. They wanted him to be different, to be someone else. This was an impossibility—he could only be himself.

The father of this young man was a large, athletic man. The son was lean, slight, a student and a lover of music. The two men were opposites. The boy said he wanted his father to accept his interests, to care about what he was doing. He told me, "I wasn't his kind of person. I would have to say that he considered me a burden. Sometimes he looked at me as if he hated me. There were times when he hesitated to introduce me to his friends as his son."

He went on to tell me how empty things felt in his home and of the many ways he attempted to gain the approval of his father. He said, "I would have given everything I owned to have him give me a hug and tell me I was a good kid. He never did." After a while, the boy stopped trying. He accepted the rejection of his father as final. He was a disappointment to his own parents. He felt he was worthless. This rejection brought depression. It usually does.

It is a humiliating experience to see disappointment in the eyes of those you love. To seek approval and see disappointment instead borders on the unbearable.

Handling Rejection   How are we to handle rejection? How can we experience it and yet avoid chronic depression?

In the Scriptures, we have the prophecy of a man with great spiritual insight, Isaiah. He spoke prophetically of the Lord Jesus Christ: His coming, the kind of man He would be, and some of the experiences He would face and endure. He described Him as a "man of sorrows and one acquainted with grief" and predicted that His would be a life of suffering (*see* Isaiah 53:3–12).

In one of the great descriptive passages found in the Bible, Isaiah is describing, in considerable detail, the kind of person the Christ would be:

> For he [Christ] shall grow up before him [the Father] as a tender plant, and as a root out of a dry ground: he hath no form nor comeliness; and when we shall see him, there is no beauty that we should desire him.
>
> Isaiah 53:2

Christ would grow before the Lord God as slowly as any other child, as a tender plant, but at the same time, an aura of the miraculous would accompany Him. Christ would be as a root sprouting out of the dry ground. We know it is impossible to root anything in dry ground; water is needed, yet Jesus, the Christ, would spring up as a spiritual plant in the barren, dry, spiritual ground of Israel.

The Christ would not be a child of great beauty or physical attractiveness. There would be no halo around His head. There would be nothing about Him that would cause us to take notice of Him. The prophet continues:

> He is despised and rejected of men; a man of sorrows, and acquainted with grief: and we hid as it were our faces from him; he was despised, and we esteemed him not.
>
> Isaiah 53:3

The Son of God experienced the human emotions of being despised and rejected. What did He do? How did He manage?

First of all, He had to settle the question of identity—who He was. He did not have to play the game of trying to be someone else. Jesus was secure in the area of personal identity. Jesus of Nazareth was the Messiah. He knew that every person in Israel had a preconceived notion of what the Messiah would look like, how He would talk and what He would do. He further knew that none of these presuppositions were correct—He was unlike anyone the people had ever met.

Each Is Unique   In the same way, it is important for each of us to settle for the fact that we are particularly unique individuals. Of course, our parents would prefer that we be more like them and sometimes this does happen and sometimes it does not. Often, children who are extreme opposites of the parents experience real and total rejection. Someone must get to these children and inform them that they must not reject themselves.

Jesus was rejected because He did not measure up to what the religious leaders thought the Christ should be. They had never seen the Son of God and yet they considered themselves experts when it came to matters of identification. This was being dumb, but Jesus loved them just the same. In fact, He loved them so much that He gave His life for them.

The Lord Jesus knew He had come from the Father and had His own unique part to play to bring salvation to the world. He knew He would not be loved, approved, or appreciated by everyone. The children of Israel, those whom He dearly loved, would misunderstand Him, ridicule, despise and reject Him—even crucify Him. Knowing this is enough to depress anyone. Did it depress Jesus? Yes, at times it did—as we will see in the chapter on Unmerited Suffering.

The Supreme Lesson   The rejection of Jesus reached its zenith when He was nailed to the cross. This would be the supreme moment of reality. When people nail you to a cross, you have good reason to suspect that they don't want you around.

What do you do and say when you are hanging on a cross and have been put there by your enemies? Do you die with bitterness and resentment filling your soul? How do you handle such moments of rejection? You must do what Jesus did. Forgive the people who have rejected you, commit yourself to God, and realize that He will "make all things work together for good" (*see* Romans 8:28).

If God can take the rejection of His own Son and the Cross of Calvary and turn these very negative circumstances into the salvation of the world, He can take the worst thing that can happen to you and turn it into something great.

While hanging on the cross, Jesus turned to the Father and said, "My God, my God, why has thou forsaken me?" (*see* Matthew 27:46). What is this? Does Jesus feel rejection in the last fleeting moments of His life? Will He die accusing the Father of desertion? No! This is not a cry of despair, but on the contrary, it is an expression of supreme confidence in God despite His profound suffering. Although God had "abandoned" Jesus to acute physical and mental pain, He did not turn His face away from Him.

In this moment of seeming rejection and depression, Jesus turned to the Father in faith and courage, saying with a loud voice for all to hear: "Father, into thy hands I commend my spirit" (*see* Luke 23:46).

Here is the supreme lesson in how to deal with rejection and its ensuing feelings of depression. Don't allow depression to linger for any great length of time. Adjust your life, your situation, your thinking, and your vocabulary quickly. Place yourself in the hands of God as quickly as you can. The moment you know you are in the hands of the Lord, the pain from the rejection will begin to vanish and the depression will flee on the wings of the morning.

18
Unmerited Suffering

Only yesterday you were full of life, health, and vigor. Illness was something someone else had. Then suddenly and without warning, you find yourself in a horizontal position. Just when you least expected it, you are struck down. You react by railing fretfully at your fate. With bitterness, you resent such untimely interference and inconvenience.

Your instincts of self-preservation become much more acute. You become highly sensitized to what you once considered normal life situations. The least provocation causes you to weep. You begin to wallow in self-pity because you feel that life has dealt you a low blow. The mistakes you made on the job, at home, or in social situations stand out clearly in your mind.

You see how often you have rationalized a failure or a weakness. You see yourself dodging vital issues and running from problems. Not only have you been mortally stricken for the first time in your life, but the illness has cut you down to size by throwing a searchlight into your inner self. The inevitable result? Depression. Illness and depression go hand in hand.

Only for a Season   When a person is told he has cancer, a tumor which might easily be malignant, heart disease, multiple sclerosis, or some other devastating physical problem, it is a natural reaction to have a season of depression. Handling the depression wisely is to keep it only for a season.

You dare not allow your depression to deteriorate into helplessness—which is a sign that your depression has become chronic. Helplessness is another way of saying, "I'm licked. I'll never be able to get through this. Life is over for me."

This is not the fact if you know Jesus Christ is alive and well in our present world. The presence of the Lord Jesus Christ makes a difference. What do people do at a time of severe need or when depression rolls in like fog if they do not have a speaking acquaintance with Jesus?

Are we saying that Christians experience times of depression? Certainly! Christians live in a real world and have real problems the same as other people. Often we are floored with sicknesses and infirmities which send us reeling, but with Christ, we never have the terrible feeling of helplessness. The Lord will pick us up and help us when we are unable to help ourselves.

People who name the Name of Christ need to get themselves settled in this area. When sickness or suffering comes, I have heard people say, "I don't understand it. I have given my life to God and I thought He would take care of me and now this happens." This kind of thinking is wrong.

The sound Bible position regarding suffering is demonstrated in the story of the three Hebrew young men who were threatened by King Nebuchadnezzar. He threatened to cast them into a fiery furnace unless they bowed down and worshipped the image he had created. This was their answer:

> . . . our God whom we serve is able to deliver us from
> the burning fiery furnace, and he will deliver us out of
> thine hand, O king. But if not, be it known unto thee,

O king, that we will not serve thy gods, nor worship the golden image which thou hast set up.

Daniel 3:17, 18

Notice carefully these words of the young men: "Our God is able to deliver us. But if not, we will not worship the golden image." In other words, right is right regardless of the consequences. This is what I firmly believe. God is God regardless of the problems, sufferings, and inequities of this life. God is still God!

The Sufferings of Christ   Do you believe the Bible account of the sufferings of Christ? Were His sufferings merited or unmerited? Did He deserve death on the cross? Your answers to these questions will no doubt be: "Yes, I do believe in the sufferings of Christ as related in the Bible. I further believe His sufferings were completely unmerited and He did not deserve to die on the cross."

Then why did the Lord God allow Christ to suffer and die such an ignominious death? Why did God not come down and rescue His Son? There is no doubt the Eternal was accomplishing a great and mighty purpose through the cross and the sufferings of Christ. Let us consider the sufferings of the Son of Man. Long before He made the journey to the cross, Jesus knew suffering. In Isaiah, we read:

He is despised and rejected of men; a man of sorrows, and acquainted with grief: and we hid as it were our faces from him; he was despised, and we esteemed him not.

Isaiah 53:3

Again, in John we read that Jesus came into His own domain and lived among His chosen people (the Israelites) and His own received Him not (*see* John 1:11).

The thought of His Passion troubled Jesus and He clearly shows us that just as the cross would be frightening to us, it also frightened Him. Jesus knew every experience of human weak-

131

ness (apart from sin) that would qualify Him to be compassionate and profoundly sensitive to our weaknesses and sufferings. He cries out to the Father:

> Now is my soul troubled; and what shall I say? Father, save me from this hour: but for this cause came I unto this hour.
>
> John 12:27

When His Passion and Crucifixion became imminent to Him, Jesus began to become dismayed and distressed. He knew His hour had come. His suffering, with all the accompanying humiliations, presented itself to His mind so vividly that He became filled with anguish and fear.

Jesus was conscious of the unbelief of the Jews; He knew Judas would betray Him; He knew the scandal the apostles would cause by their behavior; and He knew the burden of sin which would be placed on Him.

Mortal Distress   As we read of the agony of Christ in the Garden of Gethsemane, we can almost feel the combat that must have raged within Him at this time.

> He took Peter, James and John with him and began to be filled with horror and deepest distress. And he said to them, "My soul is crushed by sorrow to the point of death; stay here and watch with me." He went on a little further and fell to the ground and prayed that if it were possible the awful hour awaiting him might never come. "Father, Father," he said, "everything is possible for you. Take away this cup from me. Yet I want your will, not mine." Then he returned to the three disciples and found them asleep. "Simon!" he said. "Asleep? Couldn't you watch with me even one hour? Watch with me and pray lest the Tempter overpower you. For though the spirit is willing enough, the body is weak." And he went away again and prayed, repeating his pleadings. Again he returned to them

and found them sleeping, for they were very tired. And they didn't know what to say. The third time when he returned to them he said, "Sleep on; get your rest! But no! The time for sleep has ended! Look! I am betrayed into the hands of wicked men. Come! Get up! We must go! Look! My betrayer is here!"

Mark 14:33–42 LB

At the Incarnation, Jesus had assumed a real human nature and it is in accordance with this nature that we find Him shrinking from suffering and death. Despite the repugnance of His human nature to suffering, Christ's prayer that He might be spared is conditional. His human will was in complete accord with the will of His Father.

We see Jesus returning again and again to seek comfort in the company of the apostles. This seeking and the restlessness shown in His repeated coming and going are characteristic of a person who is deeply distressed.

Let's look into the Bible again:

He walked away, perhaps a stone's throw, and knelt down and prayed this prayer: "Father, if you are willing, please take away this cup of horror from me. But I want your will, not mine." Then an angel from heaven appeared and strengthened him, for he was in such agony of spirit that he broke into a sweat of blood, with great drops falling to the ground as he prayed more and more earnestly. At last he stood up again and returned to the disciples—only to find them asleep. . . .

Luke 22:41–45 LB

Into His Passion was concentrated all possible human suffering, from betrayal by man to abandonment by God. Could anything be worse? Yet, Jesus Christ, our Lord, turned these acts of injustice into the glorious redemption of mankind. Through the cross, the world was reconciled to God. The Apostle Paul said:

And, having made peace through the blood of his cross, by him to reconcile all things unto himself; by him, I say, whether they be things in earth, or things in heaven.

Regarding the sufferings of Christ, we are told: But we see Jesus, who was made a little lower than the angels for the suffering of death, crowned with glory and honour; that he by the grace of God should taste death for every man. For it became him, for whom are all things, and by whom are all things, in bringing many sons unto glory, to make the captain of their salvation perfect through sufferings.

Hebrews 2:9, 10

Because Jesus suffered and died, this is why He is able to identify Himself with all who suffer and this is why He cannot witness suffering without being profoundly moved by divine mercy and compassion.

When the worst thing which could happen—namely, the cross—turned into the best thing which could happen to the world—its redemption—that is real mastery. It is mastery at its very best!

Facing Handicaps   This is what Christianity is all about. Christians are people who have the power of God at work within. That power working within makes them able to face any situation and make it work for good.

I have met people who had never heard the voice of God until God stopped them by laying them down on a bed of infirmity. One of the most radiant Christians I know is a woman who has been crippled for many years. Her physical problems have developed in her a bright shining inner light.

Handicaps are things that cannot be classified as sin but they do slow us in the race of life. Sins can tie you up and so can handicaps; both must be renounced in order to run our appointed course with steadiness.

My mother has been a minister of the Gospel of Jesus Christ

for many years and has been mightily used of God. As the years progressed, she became handicapped and suffered a great deal of pain in her hips and knees, so much so that she had to be confined to a wheelchair. Because of the pain, it became impossible for her to stand at a pulpit and speak.

Did she stop preaching? No, she did not. We arranged for a desk-type pulpit to be built—one that would enable her to sit while she ministered. The handicap was stripped away and the door of ministry continued to remain open.

A Positive Outlook   You can share in this same kind of experience. Take a look at your illness from a positive viewpoint. Is there anything to be gained from it? Are there lessons you can learn?

Consider the fact that by being in a horizontal position, you are relieved from the pressure of meeting the world head-on. You are relieved of responsibilities. You don't have to worry about keeping appointments or taking care of household chores or solving the complex problems of modern-day living. You have entered into a world where, perhaps for the first time, you can think soberly about your past and future. Think of it—you are being given the rarest thing in the world—a second chance.

Your illness has knocked the nonsense out of you. It has humbled you and if you're wise, you can turn your suffering into a cleansing fire that will leave you with an inner peace and serenity. You have the opportunity to forgive those who have hurt you and to learn the true meaning of friendship through those who are standing by you.

When others see that you have merged your suffering in His, truly the Son of God will be glorified. Paul tells us this:

> Always bearing about in the body the dying of the Lord Jesus, that the life also of Jesus might be made manifest in our body.
>
> 2 Corinthians 4:10

If you can look upon your illness as a blessing in disguise, accept it and determine to make the most of it, you can be sure that God will bring this season to a close and cause the sun to shine again. Your condition as you find it today is not hopeless —not as long as there is a God in heaven, and there is! Jesus is alive to do something about it and believe me, He can.

The resurrection of Jesus from the dead became the key message of the apostles of Christ. The Bible says:

> And with great power gave the apostles witness of the resurrection of the Lord Jesus: and great grace was upon them all.
>
> Acts 4:33

These men were not simply giving mental assent to the doctrine of the resurrection but they were stating that the resurrection of Jesus from the dead meant that Christ was a contemporary figure in their present real world. They said that Jesus was alive and with them and was yet able to do all the things He had done prior to His death, burial and resurrection. In fact, even more.

Your case, your illness, your infirmity is not a hopeless situation. Don't allow yourself the false luxury of depression. Turn to the risen Christ and trust in Him with all your heart. Jesus Christ makes a difference.

If you find yourself in depression, feed your mind with the facts that this "season of heaviness" (see 1 Peter 1:6) is simply that: it is a season and it will soon be gone. The sun is going to shine again for you. Your case is not hopeless. Jesus Christ is risen from the dead!

Using Suffering   Many infirmities and diseases are healed, but not all. Some people will have to wait for the cure until the final resurrection. It is a fact that our mortal frame will eventually break down in a mortal world. We are not constructed to remain here eternally.

Yet there is no hardship or problem which comes into a life which cannot be used for good. There is no pain, no suffering, no frustration, no disappointment, that cannot be either cured or used for betterment. In Christianity, one is either healed or enriched by suffering. It is never without reason. Suffering can be of great value to us when we discover that it can be as purifying as fire as well as educational.

By having faith in God's plan for your life, you can endure suffering even though it may be very difficult and very painful. God reserves suffering for His servants whom He loves and of whom He is very proud.

> My son, despise not the chastening of the Lord; neither be weary of his correction: For whom the Lord loveth he correcteth; even as a father the son in whom he delighteth.
>
> Proverbs 3:11, 12

Peter rejoiced in sharing in the sufferings of Christ:

> But rejoice, inasmuch as ye are partakers of Christ's sufferings; that, when his glory shall be revealed, ye may be glad also with exceeding joy. [He continues:] Yet if any man suffer as a Christian, let him not be ashamed; but let him glorify God on this behalf.
>
> 1 Peter 4:13, 16

Some years ago, a young man of my acquaintance was told he had terminal cancer. Almost immediately, he set out to finish college and did receive his degree while propped up in his hospital bed during the last days of his life.

Some would say, "That was a useless thing to do." No, it was not useless. The young man was better prepared for eternity. He believed in eternal life through Christ Jesus. His suffering was used to prepare himself for his great homecoming with the Lord.

19
Failure

We live in a highly competitive society which places a high premium on success. Because of this, many of us will fail to reach the goals we have set for ourselves.

Often, failure will be the result of setting goals that are unrealistically high and completely unattainable. We have all experienced this kind of failure in one area of life or another. When we fail in an undertaking we consider especially important, we begin to experience strong feelings of inferiority and self-devaluation.

Because money means a great deal in terms of status and security, a financial loss or the loss of a job can lead to severe depression. "Keeping up with the Joneses" may cause us to continually compare our achievements and possessions with those of others. When we look at our job, our home, our social status, and our material possessions, we become envious of those who have more than we have. The personal status in society that we would like to achieve becomes something less than we think it should be. Again—depression.

Personal Limitations   Our personal limitations can also be responsible for feelings of failure. Personal characteristics which are admired by society tend to put us in a position where we compare ourselves with others. In the areas of physical appearance, intelligence, sex, special talents or abilities, few of us can find such comparisons highly satisfactory.

Instead of making the most of the assets we do have, we spend our time concentrating on our big noses, freckles, receding hairlines, and so on. Our own assets may be much greater than we realize and we can make use of our full potential if we will accept ourselves as we are.

Feelings of guilt accompany feelings of failure. We may feel we are being punished because we took advantage of our friends, or that we have shown hostility or selfishness toward those we love, or we have failed to live up to our own ethical and moral standards. When depression takes over, we drum up our own guilt feelings by going back into our past life and searching out exaggerated failures and mistakes.

The Fear of Success   In my years of counseling, I have dealt with a number of people who are deeply mixed up about the matters of success and failure and the way the two relate to the Kingdom of God. Some Christians are frightened to death of success because of the inevitable failure and punishment which they vaguely see in the offing. Others have been taught that success and pride somehow go together and the Lord is not too highly pleased with either.

Consequently, individuals who fear success become failure-prone and avoid success with precision. In time, these people will become depressed because they are going against the law of their own being. Methodically, they are destroying their self-image, their true value, and their creativity.

People who remain in depression for considerable lengths of time become particularly sensitive to any personal weaknesses they may have. A small insignificant obstacle becomes an impossible barrier and a simple difficulty in dealing with a problem is interpreted as being a total failure.

A person who becomes a depressive through failure or other reasons is not to be confused with the person who is negative or pessimistic by nature. A pessimist is primarily a person who is negative and cynical about the world in general, while a depressive is one who is negative and cynical about his own personal actions.

Depression Follows Failure   That depression follows failure is inevitable. This is the way it is. This is the way we are made. Some people unwisely wallow in their feelings of depression until they have convinced themselves they are failures, always have been failures, and always will be failures.

There are some depressives who feel they bear an invisible tattoo which reads: I'M A BORN LOSER. After a period of time, many of them really believe this and depression becomes their way of life. For this reason, we must be careful that we do not allow our periods of depression to be prolonged.

Depression usually dissipates with time. For example, when a man's wife dies, he may be depressed for several days, several months, or even several years. Time *does* heal and eventually the pain suffered by the loss of a loved one will begin to diminish.

One of the most tragic aspects of suicide is that if the person could have waited a while longer, the depression might well have lifted. Severe depressives take their own lives because they feel helpless to do anything about their condition and situation.

The Art of Forgiveness   One of the reasons that some people fall into deep depression following failure is that they have never really learned the art of forgiveness. A person who cannot forgive others will find it difficult to forgive himself for his failures. Christianity should and must shine in the realm of forgiveness. Christianity means being Christlike and being Christlike is the best thing that can be said about anyone.

The greatest prayer ever uttered was, "Father, forgive them; for they know not what they do." These words were Jesus' prayer when He was hanging on the cross, placed there by His enemies in spite of the fact that He had done no wrong.

The men who hung Jesus on that cross were wrong, dead wrong, and they should have been asking Jesus to forgive and forget the whole thing. Instead, they were jeering, taunting, and ridiculing Him. This would have been the perfect time and place for Jesus to come down from that cross and "zap" them good and proper. Jesus could have taught them a lesson they would never forget but, instead, we find Him in the spirit of complete forgiveness.

The Extreme Payoff   Jesus lived by His own rules. Some time prior to His Crucifixion, the Apostle Peter had come to Jesus with the question, "How often do you forgive a man when he deliberately sins against you and does you dirt? Seven times?"

The Lord's answer was, "Not seven times, but seventy times seven." (*See* Matthew 18:21, 22.)

140

Four hundred ninety times? This is ridiculous! Why should we be asked to do such an unrealistic thing? The reason: if you become unforgiving in your spirit, it will backfire on you. The day will come when you won't be able to forgive, even if you want to. You will further find that the Lord God will not forgive you, and in time, you will not even be able to forgive yourself. This is the extreme payoff.

In the Book of Ephesians, we find these words:

> And be ye kind one to another, tenderhearted, forgiving one another, even as God for Christ's sake hath forgiven you.
>
> Ephesians 4:32

Every true Christian has been forgiven a tremendous debt of sin by the Lord God. Consequently, we must follow the actions of the Lord, and because God forgives, we must forgive—over and over again. We forgive those who sin against us and we forgive ourselves when we are weak, make mistakes, and experience dismal failure.

No Room for Self-Pity   There is not a person in the entire world who has not tasted failure of one kind or another and the inevitable feelings of depression that follow. Most of us snap out of it in a short time and are on our way to try again or to seek some other course of action. I wish I could have said that all of us do this, but this would not be fact. Far too many depressives allow themselves the destructive luxury of diving into the lake of self-pity.

Christians who have the Spirit of Jesus living within them must be told that there is no self-pity in the Spirit of Jesus. As He was on His way to the cross, Jesus told the grief-stricken daughters of Jerusalem, "Weep not for me" (*see* Luke 23:28). There was no self-pity in Jesus and there can be no self-pity in the Christian's makeup.

Whenever you experience failure and feelings of self-pity come rolling into your mind and emotions, surrender them quickly into the hands of Christ. Surrender the impulse to feel sorry for yourself. Surrender all feelings of inferiority and help-lessness as quickly as you can. Don't harbor them for a moment longer than necessary.

Sometimes it feels good to be sorry for yourself. After all, who will feel sorry for you if you don't? Don't even allow yourself to think this way. It is a luxury you cannot afford. Many depressives carry a mark of self-pity. It is branded into their character and emotions. In time, people shun them and this further proves to the depressive that he or she is a born loser.

Our Self-Esteem   The redemption provided for us in Christ Jesus gives us a sense of self-esteem such as we have never known. There is no feeling in the world as great as the feeling which comes with the knowledge that the Lord God thought we were worth something. In fact, God valued us so much that He sent His Son to die for us.

An individual who has been truly born again can square his shoulders and stand with poise because he knows that Christ loved him and gave Himself for him. This isn't all. With the coming of the Holy Spirit, we are continually stimulated and made creative so we can be blessed people in this age and in the age to come.

> . . . Thou shalt love the Lord thy God with all thy heart, and with all thy soul, and with all thy strength, and with all thy mind; and thy neighbour as thyself.
>
> Luke 10:27

As long as you love the Lord with your whole being and your neighbor as yourself, you won't have many problems with pride and you will be able to handle success as it comes along.

Being Overcautious   Some men I have counseled with are overly cautious about becoming top executives. They are afraid that success will bring some kind of disaster to them or that it will bring failure. The fear of failure is so acute that these men are willing to pass up many golden opportunities. They endeavor to disguise their fear by saying, "I'm not sure this promotion is the will of God. I just can't seem to see the mind of the Lord in this matter. I am confused and I really need help." The quandary of what to do causes them to experience real times of depression.

My question to them usually is, "Do you think the Lord would be pleased with you if you were a failure?" The reply they give is, "No, I don't think He would be pleased with me if I were a failure, but I can't get it into my head that He would be pleased if I became a success."

The dilemma here is real. Yet, even while they are speaking, they are instinctively rejecting the idea that God wants them to settle for mediocrity.

Others try to solve this predicament by playing games of concealment. The Lord is blessing them financially but they attempt to hide it. They feel they must not stand out too much or really enjoy what they have. This kind of thinking is disruptive and destructive.

Settle it! The Lord takes no pleasure in a man's failures. When the Lord God speaks of His people, He refers to them in terms of priests, kings, overcomers, rulers. Furthermore, the Lord is not jealous of our success. He delights when His people prosper. David expresses God's desires for His people:

> Blessed is the man that walketh not in the counsel of the ungodly, nor standeth in the way of sinners, nor sitteth in the seat of the scornful. But his delight is in the law of the Lord; and in his law doth he meditate day and night. And he shall be like a tree planted by the rivers of water, that bringeth forth his fruit in his season; his leaf also shall not wither; and whatsoever he doeth shall prosper.
>
> Psalms 1:1–3

Whatsoever he doeth shall prosper. This doesn't sound like God desiring failure for His people.

The Mark of the Christian   Failure brings depression. The Lord God does not desire His children to be depressives.

143

Depressives are a problem to themselves and to God. Please settle this!

The mark of the Christian who is enjoying life, living, God, himself, and others, is joy—a deep effervescent joy. The Bible says: ". . . the joy of the Lord is your strength" (Nehemiah 8:10). It's impossible to have the joy of the Lord in your soul and be depressed at the same time. The two are not compatible. When you are full of joy, your food tastes good, life has zest and meaning, promotion is taken in stride, and failure, with its subsequent depression, will simply be a part of the total fabric of life.

If you continue to live and act as a person in this real world of ours, you are sure to experience failure of one kind or another. So what! People are too busy striving for the same things that you are to be concerned with your failures. Learn from the mistakes you did make and spotlight your efforts on your positive qualities. Your failure may be a blessing in disguise.

Forgive yourself for being dumb and for being a failure. Place yourself and your circumstances into the hands of the Lord. Walk away as fast as you can from your self-pity. Draw on the resources of God made available to you through the person of the Holy Spirit and allow the continued joy of the Lord to be your strength.

20
Old Age

Next to dying, recognizing that we are aging can be the most profound shock we can experience in our lifetime. With the findings of modern medicine, the span of life is increasing with every year. We have more senior citizens today than ever before. In fact, there are four times more people in this country over sixty-five than there were in 1900.

If the present rate of aging continues, there will be over twenty-six million senior citizens by 1980. This amounts to 15 percent of the total population. Because of these statistics, facing up to age is a vital part of facing up to life.

I am not an old man but day by day I am on my way. I certainly want to practice what I preach to others. To this point in my life, I have thoroughly and completely enjoyed living. I have a zest for life. I have a spark in me which causes me to enjoy meeting people, going places, and doing things. I love life.

Since old age is part of life, I look forward to what the future years have to offer. I also realize that my future happiness depends largely on what I have learned during the years already behind me. For this reason, I must live every day to the best of my ability. David said in the Psalms:

> The righteous shall flourish like the palm tree: he shall grow like a cedar in Lebanon. Those that be planted in the house of the Lord shall flourish in the courts of our God. They shall still bring forth fruit in old age; they shall be fat and flourishing; To shew that the Lord is upright: he is my rock, and there is no unrighteousness in him.
>
> Psalms 92:12–15

Since the Bible clearly states that there is a way to live which will make old age fruitful, I want to find this way for myself so that I can help others to do the same. There's no need to settle for less than the best.

The Senior Citizens   In our day, we face a peculiar situation. The average length of life for men is sixty-five years; for women, it is seventy. We have such a great number of aged people with us that the label of senior citizen has been coined in our generation.

Because people are living longer than at any other time in history, the mastery of old age is not only a pressing necessity, it is imperative that we find the secret of making old age fruitful. Sad to say, for many people old age is a tragic burden instead of a blessing. They are coming to the end of life all frayed and frustrated.

I have visited places in our country where older people gather together and I have not liked what I saw. In St. Petersburg, Florida and Long Beach, California, I saw the aged gathered to spend their last days. For the most part, these people represent the economically stable, for they have been able to sell their properties, leave the old hometowns, and put down their roots elsewhere.

Financially, they are not in need but most of them have been totally unrealistic. In their dreams, they have imagined Florida or California to be a heaven on earth, the ideal place in which to spend their latter years. Too many of them have ended up disillusioned and frustrated. They have divorced themselves from all useful activities, from all that is meaningful in life, and they have tried to settle down to a life which is void of significance. Oh, they are busy—busy trying to keep busy! For them, life has lost all value. They live a trivial existence of nothingness while waiting for the end of life to come. This is tragic. It is a waste of precious lives which could be fruitful.

The Answer to the Dilemma   Is there an answer to this dilemma of old age? More and more senior-citizen communities are being planned and built—but this is not the answer. What is the alternative? We need not search far to find the answer.

On the day of Pentecost, when the church of Jesus Christ was born, the elderly were not excluded from the plan and purpose of God. Rather, they were very much included! When the Apostle Peter stood up to address the multitude after they were visited by the Holy Spirit, he said:

> But this is that which was spoken by the prophet Joel;
> [See Joel 2:28, 29.] And it shall come to pass in the last
> days, saith God, I will pour out of my Spirit upon all
> flesh: and your sons and your daughters shall prophesy,
> and your young men shall see visions, and your old
> men shall dream dreams: And on my servants and on

my handmaidens I will pour out in those days of my
Spirit, and they shall prophesy.

Acts 2:16–18

Notice carefully these words taken from the Book of Joel which
Peter spoke by the inspiration of the Holy Spirit: . . . *your old
men shall dream dreams.* Here we learn that God by the Holy
Spirit does not relegate the aged to a realm of nothingness.
Dreaming does not require physical ability or strength. Therefore, up to the very end of life, people can have a clear insight
into the purposes of God.

When the Apostle Paul wrote to Timothy, his son in the
Gospel, he instructed him not to enroll a widow who is under
sixty years of age (*see* 1 Timothy 5:9). This age would be comparable to about eighty years today, considering the average life-
span then and now. Seemingly, it has never been the plan of
God for people to retire at a compulsory age, sit down, and do
nothing. However, this is how it is today. When we reach the
early sixties, we are forced to retire from our jobs. What do we
do then?

Life Must Have Meaning   The answer to this frustrating
predicament is found in the Word of God. We dare not settle
into the rut of the material realm of just earning a living while
we are young. If the primary purpose of life becomes the gain-
ing of material possessions, then when this endeavor stops, all
meaning in life stops with it. Our lives must take on more
meaning every day we live. Life must include more than a
day-by-day existence to earn a living and save a few dollars for
old age.

As Christians, each one of us must build a controlling purpose
into our lives. Everyone who names the Name of Christ, young
and old, must be an evangel of the Gospel in one way or another. From the obligation of being a living testimony for
Christ, there is no retirement. This is a lifetime job.

John Wesley never retired. He was busy right to the very end
telling everybody everywhere, "I commend my Saviour to

you." The Apostle Paul never retired and let the rest of the world go by. Some of his last words were:

> As for me, I feel that the last drops of my life are being poured out for God. The time for my departure has arrived. The glorious fight that God gave me I have fought, the course that I was set I have finished, and I have kept the faith. The future for me holds the crown of righteousness which the Lord, the true judge, will give to me in that day—and not, of course, only to me but to all those who have loved what they have seen of him.
>
> 2 Timothy 4:6–8 PHILLIPS

You will have to agree that Paul did master old age. His latter years were fruitful, blessed years, full of meaning and value.

Premium on Youth   One of the problems of our day is the exaggerated emphasis on youth. Everything in our society is geared toward youth. Our style of dress, our entertainment, sports, movies, and commercials all put the emphasis on being young. The import laid upon perpetual youth is a misinterpretation of normal living.

The elderly are given little or nothing to help them in making critical adjustments in areas of decreasing physical health, retirement, reduced income, and the death of a spouse. Age is treated as though it were a plague which must be avoided at all costs.

Age should be revered, not despised. It cannot be ignored nor *should* it be ignored for it has much to offer in wisdom gained by years of experience. Today, the people who should offer the solidity of maturity to young people act as if they had never grown up themselves! Mothers resent motherhood and parade around like miniskirted kids. This should not be. Is it any wonder that the young people have no respect for their elders?

We need the experience of age. We should listen to age more than we do. Experienced elders are needed in the churches of our day, but sad to say, the real true ministry of the elder is vanishing rapidly. People are retiring from the service of the church at approximately the same time they retire from their jobs. This is a big mistake. Usually, they retire to a life of emptiness when they would have more time and opportunity to do the work of the Lord. This is tragic!

If old age is to be dignified and beautiful, we must bring into it something which makes it beautiful. We do not grow old—we become old by not growing. If we will obey and not resist the laws of growth, these laws will continue to operate until the end of life and beyond.

Life From Within   We cannot stay the process of getting old but we can continue to live a worthwhile life. The various subterfuges of dress and paint cannot stop age. Age stares right through such flimsy stuff. Painting a dead tree with green paint does not make it alive nor does it fool anyone. Life comes from within. If there is no life within, there is no life at all.

In the last years of my father's life (he died at eighty-six) there were days when his age, limitations, and depressions began to show. He would say to me, "Jim, I don't feel old inside but I can't seem to get anything done. I'm exhausted before I begin. This old age business is getting to me."

Dad's depressions didn't last very long because he instinctively knew how to handle them. He shifted his eyes from himself and his limitations and became involved in what he could do. Dad and I lived on the same street and I would, of necessity, have to drive by his home on my way to and from work. Most of the time, the garage door would be open and he would be working away on some project—usually with real difficulty. Because his eyesight was failing, some of his projects didn't turn out too well, but nevertheless, they were being done and he was doing something. He was living and leading an active life.

Despite his physical limitations, he was a rugged individual who knew that life was worth living and so long as there was life in him, he would continue to be active. He would not allow the word *helpless* to become a part of his vocabulary. Consequently, he was never a man who became a depressive, especially over the matter of old age.

149

Feelings of Helplessness   I contrast Dad with another man I know. He is perhaps ten years younger, but when he retired from his job he did so with the feeling that he had become an old man. The depression of becoming an old man hit him like a ton of bricks.

This man now spends his days wrapped in a sweater in front of the television set—waiting to die. He is helpless. He cannot paint the house trim, clean the garage, wash a dish in the kitchen, or sweep a floor. He simply can't do anything because he feels he is too old!

He is no such thing. He is not helpless, but he has made himself helpless. He feels there is nothing in life to live for. He is old and depressed about it. This depression has become his permanent attitude. He doesn't want to change. This is regrettable.

The problem of this man is compounded by the fact that he is driving his wife right up the wall. She is depressed because of his actions and attitude. Presently, there are two depressed people dying with one another. This is a dead-end street where no one wins or survives.

His wife is now saying that she is helpless to change the situation. So—two people sit in their helplessness when, in reality, they are not. If they will open their lives to the divine invasion of the Lord Jesus Christ, their feelings of helplessness will leave. They can begin to live again.

What Lies Ahead   Just because we have ceased to grow physically does not mean we have stopped growing altogether. There can be in all of us a wonderful mental and spiritual development so long as we live, even after physical growth has ceased. It is a grave and fatal mistake to assume that a physical standstill or even regression means the end of all growth.

This is not true. Sometimes God allows the pain of a slight ailment in old age just to arouse us to more carefulness in a more important area. As we become more disciplined in general by caring for the one ailment, we tone up our general health. In this way, we live longer.

A good rule which should be adopted by all of us as we grow older is to strive to subdue the weak areas of our personality. By

150

becoming conscious of present negative traits, we can see what we will be like in later years. Our abnormal characteristics will become magnified as we begin to age. If we are rigid in our outlook, obstinate, have narrowed interests, are overconscientious, and bigoted, or if we are in any way handicapped psychologically, we will be especially vulnerable to psychoses in old age.

Another good thing to remember is to spend less time looking into the realm of memory and more time looking forward to the possibilities which lie ahead. Remember Paul saying:

> My brothers, I do not consider myself to have grasped it fully even now. But I do concentrate on this: I forget all that lies behind me and with hands outstretched to whatever lies ahead I go straight for the goal—my reward the honour of my high calling by God in Christ Jesus.
>
> Philippians 3:13,14 PHILLIPS

Recently, I read an account examining the careers of some 400 men. All were notable and outstanding in various fields— statesmen, artists, warriors, poets, writers. The account showed that the decade between 60 and 70 years contained 35 percent of the world's greatest achievements; between 70 and 80, 23 percent; after 80, 8 percent. In other words, 64 percent of the greatest achievements have been accomplished by men who passed their sixtieth year.

Stir Up the Gift   With all this in mind, the next words are directed to those who are over sixty years of age and who have ceased being creative within the ranks of the church. You are only finished with your ministry in God as you allow yourself to be finished. Today, you can again stir up the gift of God which is in you and become of value to the church of Jesus Christ. The church needs you—you need the church. Don't be a quitter. Don't leave the church in the inexperienced hands of youth, for you have much to offer.

Don't allow things in the church to go downhill simply because you feel you have done your part and it is time for you to relax and retire. Keep active. In so doing, you continue to increase and grow. If you cease to give out, you cease to increase. The eternities to come will be centuries of continual growth and development in Jesus Christ. I expect to know far more of God and His wonderful ways in the milleniums to come than I know today. This is growth!

I once read of some old Quakers who, when they had a good year of spiritual growth, were allowed to add one-fourth of an inch to the brim of their broad hats. Among the American Indians of the West Coast, there is a custom that allows them to sit in the front row of the church if they had a good week spiritually; if a bad week, at the rear; if a mediocre week, then halfway back! The pastor can tell at a glance the spiritual temperature of each one of his parishioners.

The best indication of growth is not a broader brim on a hat or a front-row seat in church but an expanding mind and front-seat soul—one eager for truth and continuous growth. How do you gain with the years? Don't retire—simply change your occupation. In your later years, take the opportunity to do what you have always wanted to do—be an evangel for the Lord Jesus Christ!

21
Death

When death strikes down someone very near and dear to us, the devastating effects of depression must also be dealt with. Depression is common when death comes to someone we love. Mourning over our loss is natural. Death is real and must be faced as a natural part of the human situation.

Too often, death is dressed up in artificial clothes and takes on the appearance of something unreal. This can be mentally damaging. Many of our funeral and burial customs border on the absurd. We embalm so the person will not appear dead. We talk of sleep instead of death. Mourning is not considered sophisticated so emotions are bottled up.

In our changing society, we don't really know what is expected of us—how we are supposed to feel—and it could well be that eventually we arrive at a state of feeling nothing. To live without deep feelings is a catastrophe. Feelings and emotions are to be tasted and experienced. This is true of the emotions surrounding death.

Living With Death   We live with death through our entire lifetime. As children, we are told not to play in the street or we might be hit by a car and die. "Don't climb that tree—you'll fall and kill yourself!" We know death is there if we are not careful.

We talk about death—but not too much. It doesn't make us feel very comfortable. Yet, why not talk about it? What are we afraid of? Perhaps, if we brought the matter of death out into the light and discussed it, we would not have the very common problem of depression concerning death.

I don't enjoy talking of death any more than you do and I am not implying that talking about it will eliminate the feelings which surround death. The emotions associated with death will hit you full in the face and maybe even knock you flat on your back, but if you know what you ought to know about death, you will not remain in your helplessness.

Christianity has the only real answers about death. This is not an oversimplification. It is the truth.

Jesus Speaks of Death   The Christian faith lights up that dark area of life—death—and it lights it up with more than words. The light of the Christian faith is Jesus who came into our world as a man and spoke of death as a man who knew something about it. Jesus knew He was going to die but He was not afraid of it. Read His words carefully:

Even as the Son of man came not to be ministered unto, but to minister, and to give his life a ransom for many.

Matthew 20:28

Therefore doth my Father love me, because I lay down my life, that I might take it again. No man taketh it from me, but I lay it down of myself. I have power to lay it down, and I have power to take it again. This commandment have I received of my Father.

John 10:17,18

This sounds as if Jesus knew something about death which the average person does not know. Death did not frighten Jesus. He knew a real death awaited Him but He fully realized that death was only going to open a new world. Jesus died but He did not stay dead.

Recently, I read of a certain order of monks who sit in a circle and as the name of each one is called, he answers, "Present." Then the names of the deceased members of the order are called and someone answers, "Present." When the name of Jesus Christ is called, they all answer, "Present." These monks have laid hold of a vital and important truth and are illustrating it with wisdom and simplicity. Jesus Christ died but He is risen and present wherever there are two or three gathered in His Name.

I had rather be wrong with Jesus than right with anyone else! Jesus affirmed and illustrated life after death. I sink or swim with Him!

The Damascus Road At the time of his journey along the Damascus road, a man named Saul (Paul) was apprehended by the risen Christ (*see* Acts 9:1–9). Prior to this meeting, Saul fully believed that Jesus was an impostor, a blasphemer, and that He had died as all heretics should die. To Saul, up to the time of encounter, Jesus was nothing but a dead Jew.

Suddenly, Saul's entire world went into eclipse. A great light shone out of the heavens, blinded him, and as he fell to the ground, he heard a voice speaking to him in the Hebrew language, saying, "Saul, Saul, why do you persecute me?"

Saul was dumbfounded as he asked, "Who are you, Lord, that I persecute you?" The voice said, "I am Jesus whom thou persecutest." Jesus was alive! That fact transformed Saul from a tangled-up, unhappy persecutor to a free and happy proclaimer of the Good News—the Gospel of salvation through the Lord Jesus Christ.

From the time of this initial meeting, Jesus Christ remained with Paul-Saul for the rest of his natural life and is presently with him in the heavenlies. The words of Jesus, "Lo, I am with you always, even unto the end of the ages" (see Matthew 28:20) became a lifeline for Paul.

The risen Christ, in the person of the Holy Spirit, came to dwell within the inner life of Paul and Paul knew it. From the moment Jesus Christ came to live within him, Paul was never again alone.

Knowing Jesus is in you and with you raises the level of depression when death invades the circle of your family and friends. Of course, there will be some depression. It is bound to come in a time of mourning and sorrow but it will not remain to cloud your life continually.

In a little while your mourning will be turned to joy and singing again. How can we be sure of this? Jesus is alive and dwelling within us and, because He is alive, the day will come when those we love who have died in Christ will also be alive again.

Christ's Duel With Death People coming to life again? Yes! Let me tell you about it. . . . When Jesus died, He knew His death would be for a set period of time. He was not going to remain in death. Death would not be the end of life and existence for Him.

Jesus said He was giving His generation a sign. As Jonah had been in the belly of the fish for three days and nights and then came out of the fish alive, so He would die, be entombed, and spend three days and nights in the heart of the earth. Then He said He would rise from the dead. What Jesus said would happen *did* happen. After three days and nights of being dead, He came out of the grave alive—raised from the dead by the Spirit of holiness.

Jesus faced death, experienced death, and talked about death without a trace of depression. He knew physical death was not the end of life. Jesus knew and taught that the soul and spirit of a man go on living after his heart has stopped.

The disciples of Jesus fell into deep depression at the time of the death of Christ because they did not know and understand the truths of the resurrection of the dead. Their understanding of life, death, and the resurrection was completely changed when Jesus Christ rose from the dead, appeared to them and showed himself alive by many infallible proofs. They knew now that a man or woman could die and come back to life again—raised from the dead by the power of God.

Our Resurrection   The disciples further learned the truth of the Second Coming of the Lord Jesus Christ. This means that Jesus Christ is going to come back to this earth, bodily, physically, as the glorified man, Christ Jesus.

When He returns, the moment will be marked by a tremendous event—the resurrection of Christians and all the saints of ages past. The Bible talks about this moment of resurrection in no uncertain terms.

> For if we believe that Jesus died and rose again, even so them also which sleep in Jesus will God bring with him. For this we say unto you by the word of the Lord, that we which are alive and remain unto the coming of the Lord shall not prevent them which are asleep. For the Lord himself shall descend from heaven with a shout, with the voice of the archangel, and with the trump of God: and the dead in Christ shall rise first: Then we which are alive and remain shall be caught up together with them in the clouds, to meet the Lord in the air: and so shall we ever be with the Lord.
>
> 1 Thessalonians 4:14–17

Christians will not remain dead indefinitely. No! Christians will remain in death only for a set period of time—from the moment of their death to the moment of the return of Christ.

This is precisely why a true Christian does not mourn in the same way as other people of the world. We mourn, yes! We mourn because we have lost a person of value, a companion, a friend—and our life must undergo adjustment. However, we do not mourn as those who have no hope. We have hope of the resurrection. We shall see, meet, love, and live with those who have died before us and have gone into the presence of the Lord.

We are going to live again in a brand-new social order where sin, sickness, sorrow, and death have been eliminated. This is what we anticipate and believe. Believing this is the remedy for depression which accompanies death. We are depressed, but not for long.

Being in Christ and having the hope of the resurrection ringing in your soul will keep you from becoming a depressive as a result of death invading your human situation. Being in Christ means eternal life. Eternal life means that your life as a person continues after physical life comes to an end.

Facing Up to Death   To those who have recently lost a loved one, may I address these next words? You have just experienced an extremely traumatic loss but the severity of the shock will depend upon your personality makeup. The more stable and integrated your personality is, the more readily you will adjust to your loss. If you are an unstable individual, you will find adjustment very difficult.

Recently, a woman of my acquaintance lost her husband in death at the height of his career. He was a good man and they were a devoted couple. Her world broke into a thousand pieces when she was told he had died. What would she do? How could she face the world? What was to become of her? The woman fell into deep depression and remained there for a number of years. Any conversation with her would inevitably include her dead husband and one detail of their life after another would be repeated over and over again.

157

One of her major problems was that for their entire married life she had no identity of her own. She was always known as Mrs. So-and-So. Her total life had been given to her husband to serve him, and this she did with gladness. This was good, but not good enough.

God never intended that marriage should be the total merging of one personality into another until one of the personalities would become completely indistinguishable. Marriage is the blending of two personalities, with each adding his or her best to the total relationship. As time went on, the woman fell into such depression that she felt people did not like her for herself. She believed that she had only been accepted into her church and social circle because of her husband.

In time, and through the help of good friends, her bereavement began to diminish gradually. She discovered she was a unique and individual person. She found she could really perform tasks that made life worthwhile and meaningful. Slowly, but surely, she walked out of her depression. Today, she is a vibrant individual who travels, visits the sick and has a new lease on life. This woman found out that life is worth living even after the central person in her life had been taken from her in death. She now knows that the living can keep on living.

There are many persons who never fully recover from bereavement. In some instances, they lose the will to live and die themselves within a short time.

Overcoming Bereavement   To help you overcome your bereavement, there are several things you should be aware of. First of all, as a person who has lost a loved one, you are grief-stricken and since grief is a safety valve which God has given to you, feel free to express it. Trying to be brave under such circumstances is not being honest with yourself.

Complete honesty on your part demands that you face the fact that death has occurred and that you must go on from there. When friends and relatives come to pay their respects, talk to them about your loved one. Try to re-create a living picture of the person as you knew him in the fullness of life.

Tears are a normal, healthy way to express grief. If you stifle them because of embarrassment, your grief will descend more crushingly upon you when you are alone. Remember, repressing grief is bad for you.

The death of a loved one is almost always accompanied by very intense guilt feelings. It is perfectly natural to experience them during this time. Whether they are justified or not is immaterial. You will feel you should have been more considerate or you should have spent more time with the deceased or you should have made fewer demands. You will find yourself saying, "If only I had done more. . . . If only I had the chance to do things over again. . . . If only I hadn't been so inconsiderate."

Yes, you will have guilt feelings but in time they will work their way out. Try to think of the nice things you have done and, when you do so, you will in all probability discover that you were a pretty good person, after all.

Isolating Yourself   Losing a loved one is bad enough but there is nothing worse for you than isolating yourself from your friends and relatives. Don't put yourself in a position to lose others as well.

One man I know lost his wife in an auto accident. He became bitter, resentful, and fell into deep and severe depression. In his black moods, he would plot the death of the person who was responsible for the accident. The death of his wife was a real tragedy to him and he would tell anyone who would listen to him that this was the case. The man became so unbearable in his attitude that he drove his children and friends away from him. His friends shunned him and in time he was left completely alone.

This man has allowed his depression to become a way of life. When you speak with him, he talks about marrying again and picking up his life where he left it, but it is only a dream. He doesn't seem to want to pick himself up. With the help of God it can be done but he has elected to keep the Lord in the background and to live in his own world of self-pity.

Life can be very cruel at times and we must remember there will be occasions when we must adjust to these cruelties and adjust quickly. The period of adjustment must be short. This is the only way we can keep depression from becoming our life's attitude.

Don't make the same mistake this man made. Keep in touch with your friends more than you did before. Make any excuse to see them. Invite them out for lunch, for shopping, for a drive, or for a friendly visit. You've suffered a deep loss. You need your friends now more than ever.

Give Yourself Away   The death of your companion or loved one is not the end of everything. There are new and interesting people to meet who can add immeasurably to your life and you can add much to theirs. Get yourself into the swing of things as soon as possible. The symbol of life is action. Visit your neighbor or friend and help him paint the garage or mow the lawn.

Don't become a selfish person and withhold your talents from those who need them. *Give yourself away.* When you are able to do things for yourself, you're on your way to overcoming grief. When you are able to do things for others, you have overcome your grief.

Your grief will run a natural course and then pass. If you allow it to leave only a vacuum, that vacuum will soon become filled with self-pity. To avoid this, start giving yourself away. Start with Christ. Give yourself to Christ—then prepare yourself for death and forget about it. Live! . . . with anticipation of what the coming eternities are going to bring.

You are just now launching out into the world of new adventures. Enjoy this new world. Your loved one who has died in Christ is having a better time than you are and is not looking down from heaven in anger because you are smiling and enjoying life. Bring your depression under your feet and stamp on it.

Each day, say to yourself, "I am going to live life fully today and prepare myself to spend eternity with Jesus Christ my Lord and those who have gone on before me."